DOING ARCHAEOLOGY

To the memory of Adan E. Treganza,
an archaeologist's archaeologist.

Point Reyes, California, from the 1965 archaeological field camp on Drake's Bay. *A. E. Treganza, pencil on cardboard.*

DOING ARCHAEOLOGY

A Cultural Resource Management Perspective

Thomas F. King

Left Coast Press Inc.

Walnut Creek, California

LEFT COAST PRESS, INC.
1630 North Main Street, #400
Walnut Creek, California 94596
http://www.LCoastPress.com

ISBN 1-59874-002-4 hardcover
ISBN 1-59874-003-2 paperback

Library of Congress Control Number 2005928675

05 06 07 08 09 5 4 3 2 1

Printed in the United States of America

♾™ The paper used in this publication meets the minimum requirements of American National Standard for Information Sciences—Permanence of Paper for Printed Library Materials, ANSI/NISO Z39.48–1992.

Contents

Preface

This book is designed to be a general introduction to the practice of archaeology—the science of the human cultural past. More specifically, it's an introduction to the practice of archaeology in the context of what's called "cultural resource management" or just "CRM" in the United States, passing under names like "management of heritage" and "protecting patrimony" in other countries. I'm assuming that the typical reader will be a college student, maybe in an introductory anthropology class, maybe in some other discipline. It's estimated that CRM is about a US$600 million industry in this early twenty-first century,[1] and the majority of students graduating from universities as archaeologists in the United States will spend at least some parts of their careers working in some aspect of CRM. So if you're a college student interested in archaeology, it's a good idea for you to read up on how CRM is practiced. If you're an instructor, I think you'll be doing your students a favor if you help them get a handle on CRM, and I hope this book will be a reasonably painless way to do so.

I hope this book will also speak to you if you're a precollege student, or not a formal student at all but just someone who wants an overview of the field, a sense of what it's like to do archaeology and maybe what you need to learn in order to do it. As I write this I also have in mind people in other lines of work who cross paths with archaeologists, have to work with them, and would like to have an idea what in the world they're about: The biologist who finds herself working with an archaeologist on an environmental impact statement, the farmer who finds an archaeologist—or somebody who says he's an archaeologist—knocking at the door wanting to walk around in the pasture and look for "sites."

Or perhaps you're someone whose ancestors, or special places, are interesting to archaeologists, and you're wondering why, or what you ought to do about it. Maybe archaeologists are asking—or neglecting to ask—permission to look for or excavate places associated with your community's past, or maybe you're wondering whether and how it might be useful to you to work with archaeologists to protect or learn about such places. I hope this book can help you figure out what the archaeologists are up to, whether you ought to cooperate with them, how your interests may coincide or differ.

You may be a practitioner of a discipline other than archaeology that does "CRM," or historic preservation, or something of the kind. Maybe you're an architectural historian, or some other kind of historian, or a planner, a landscape architect, a historical architect, or a geographer, cultural anthropologist, sociologist, or folklife specialist. If you're in one of these fields, you may find yourself teaming up with, or contending with, archaeologists in your work. I hope this book will help you figure out what they're about.

Or maybe you're trying to build something—a highway, a housing project, a farm pond—and a government agency is telling you that you need to hire an archaeologist or "CRM firm" to do a "survey" before they can release money to help you or issue you a permit. Maybe you work for a government agency and are trying to figure out what you have to do to comply with the cultural resource laws, or what requirements you ought to lay on somebody seeking your agency's help. Maybe you're a lawyer trying to develop a case, and you think you may need archaeologists as expert witnesses. Perhaps you're an environmental activist, or a concerned citizen, wondering if you can get some mileage out of archaeology in saving a valued place from development. You who pay the bills for cultural resource management, or just have to communicate with the people who do cultural resource management, have every right and reason to understand why you need to do it, and to develop a basis for judging what's worth buying and what's not. I hope this book will help you.

There are lots of other introductory archaeology textbooks, most of them oriented not toward cultural resource management but toward understanding archaeology as a research discipline. I'll refer to several of them later, and list some at the end. One set of books I'll refer to repeatedly is the *Archaeologist's Toolkit*, seven volumes in all, published in 2003 under the editorship of Larry Zimmerman and William Green.[2] The *Toolkit* provides lengthier and more technical discussion than I can give here about many aspects of archaeological practice, particularly in the United States, often in the context of CRM. Although there are quite a few things in the *Toolkit* with which I disagree—particularly in the ways several of its authors describe CRM and the laws that structure it—on the whole I think it's an excellent guide, and I'm not going to waste anyone's time picking nits with it. I recommend it if you want to go beyond this book and read in detail about the techniques and methods involved in doing archaeology in the United States. As we go along, I'll note specific parts of the *Toolkit* you may want to look at if you're interested in particular subjects. However, I also recommend that when you read what its authors say about CRM, take it with a grain of salt. If you want the real skinny on CRM—I won't be modest— read *my* books.[3]

Acknowledgments

No one but the author is responsible for the outlook that informs this book or the opinions and biases it expresses, but I'm grateful to R. Joe Brandon, Nancy Farrell, Chris Goodwin, Russ Kaldenberg, Claudia Nissley, and Rebecca Yamin for their contributions and advice, and to SWCA Environmental Consultants for encouragement and support.

I'm also thankful to Rob Edwards of Cabrillo College, Matt Seddon of SWCA, Steve Black of the University of Texas, and Joe Labadie of the U.S. National Park Service for sharing photos of archaeology in process; to Leaf Hillsman and the Karuk Tribal Council for permission to use a photograph of the World Renewal priest's lodge; to Arnold Nova of the Yurok Tribal Fisheries Department for permission to use the image of the 58-pound salmon; to Raymond Mattz Jr. and Sr. for permission to use their images with the same fish; and to Yurok Tribal Historic Preservation Officer Thomas Gates for putting me in touch with them. I'm also glad that my quest for illustrative material took me to the Web sites of Texas Beyond History and the Cabrillo College Archaeological Technology Program, which I'm happy to recommend to readers. My thanks also go to Bob McGimsey, Hester Davis, Jane Kellett, and Tom Green for the image of salvage archaeology in 1970, and for dropping whatever they had to drop to get it to me so promptly.

And I'm particularly honored to have this book be among the first products of Left Coast Press, Inc., and am indebted to the Press, its owner Mitch Allen, and editor Virginia Hoffman of Last Word Editorial Services for making its production possible.

Chapter One

What's This All About?

What Is Archaeology?

Archaeology is the study of the human past, using stuff.

Four important words here. First, archaeology is a *study*—a kind of research. Second, it's about *human beings*—not dinosaurs (that's paleontology) or rock formations (that's geology), but human beings. Third, it's about human beings in the *past,* not the present or future—though the "past" can be pretty recent, and we like to think what we study is *relevant* to the present and future. Finally, what we study is *stuff*—the things that people left behind, lost, abandoned, ate, walked around on, lived in, threw at each other, as well as the stuff that made up their bodies. We also study words written on paper, transcribed electronically, and spoken into our ears, and we examine the natural environment, but the unique focus of archaeology is on stuff, and what it can tell us.

Who Are You?

I assume you're reading this because you want to know something about archaeology. Maybe you're a student; maybe you're interested in archaeology as a hobby; maybe you're thinking of doing it for a living.

Or maybe you're working in some other field—history or architecture or urban planning, perhaps—and have archaeologists as colleagues whose ways of thinking you need to figure out.

Or maybe you own a piece of property and are trying to develop it, or you work for a government agency, and you've learned that you have archaeological sites to deal with. How, you wonder, do I do this?

Or maybe you just think—like about 87.5 percent of the population, at least in the United States—that archaeology is neat.

This book is designed to be the first one you read about archaeology—or maybe the only one. But it probably isn't. At the very least, you've undoubtedly read novels that feature archaeology, or books and articles about past civilizations uncovered by archaeologists, and you've seen movies in which archaeologists find treasures from the past and have adventures doing it. You may have read quite a lot about archaeology, and about the results of archaeological research—perhaps in Egypt, or Central America, or the Andes. Or you may have worked on archaeological field projects, perhaps near your home, perhaps in other countries. If you have, a lot of what this book contains may be old news. Or maybe not, for a couple of reasons.

For one thing, this book is about *doing* archaeology, not about its results. You may have read a lot about the archaeology of Israel, or China, or western Pennsylvania, and learned about the events, people, and cultures that archaeologists in those areas have reconstructed. That's great, but what this book is about is *how* archaeologists learn such things—how the study is done, and why it's done that way.

Second, each of us archaeologists—or people, for that matter—has a particular perspective, and mine may well be different from those of the authors you've read or the archaeologists you've worked with. Which brings me to the subtitle.

What Is Cultural Resource Management?

This book is subtitled "A Cultural Resource Management Perspective." What is "cultural resource management"?

I'll go into this in Chapter Five, but in a nutshell, "cultural resource management" (CRM) is a fancy term for trying to take care of what's important to people for cultural reasons—including archaeological sites, but also including old buildings, neighborhoods, songs, stories, dance forms, religious beliefs and practices—in the context of the modern world's laws, politics, governments, and economic forces. That's my definition, anyway; others use the term differently. Almost everybody who uses the term, though—and it's used this way mostly in the United States—uses it to include doing archaeology in connection with development and land use, under various national, state or provincial, tribal, and local laws. In other words, doing archaeology in places that are in danger of being bulldozed, flooded, bombed, plowed, or otherwise screwed up, or that are managed by government agencies. That's my perspective, which is a bit different from the perspective of someone who teaches archaeology in a university or works in a museum, though many people who do that kind of work also do "CRM."

Who Am I? Pothunter to Professional

I've been doing archaeology and CRM for close to fifty years, starting in my early teens as what archaeologists call a "pothunter." That term—a derogatory one—means someone without all the proper training and credentials who digs in archaeological sites to find stuff, which he or she then keeps or sells. Typically (but not universally) a pothunter doesn't use very good techniques, so he or she may destroy a lot of stuff, and the information represented by the stuff. Typically (but not universally) a pothunter doesn't take very good notes, or publish the results of what he or she does. Typically (but not universally) the stuff a pothunter digs up doesn't go to a museum or other public institution; the pothunter keeps it, sells it, trades it, or eventually throws it away.

In my case, it didn't take me long—because I'd been reading about archaeology since I was about five years old, and wanted to be an archaeologist when I grew up—to become an unusual pothunter in that I used pretty good field methods, kept notes, wrote reports on what I did, and put my stuff in a museum. This made me, in the eyes of most archaeologists, an "amateur archaeologist." I was more or less doing archaeology; I just wasn't getting paid to do it. From there I went on to get the formal education that you need to do archaeology professionally—eventually getting a PhD from the University of California, Riverside. The PhD was in anthropology, not specifically archaeology, which is the way it works in the United States. In most of this country's academic institutions, archaeology is mostly organized as a subfield of anthropology—the general study of human beings and their culture, past and present. What is sometimes called "classical" archaeology, however—generally focusing on the study of Greek, Roman, and other

Figure 1. Salvage archaeology in Arkansas, 1970: The Keller Site—a village site over a thousand years old, with graves—is destroyed by agricultural land leveling while archaeologists from the Arkansas Archaeological Survey salvage what they can. *Photo courtesy Arkansas Archaeological Survey.*

Mediterranean civilizations—is usually lumped together with history, art history, and other disciplines called the "humanities." In the colleges and universities of some countries, archaeology is a stand-alone discipline. But if you're doing archaeology in the United States, you're almost surely going to get your advanced degree in anthropology.

While in college I began to make a living doing archaeology. The only jobs to be had in those days (the 1960s) were in "salvage archaeology"—excavating sites that were about to be destroyed by highways, dams, and other kinds of construction projects. This was interesting, often exciting, but pretty frustrating and saddening. We'd dig perhaps three or four percent of an ancient site—say, a 2,000-year-old California Indian village site or cemetery—and then the money and time would run out and the rest of the site would be bulldozed into oblivion. It hurt. So when President Lyndon Johnson signed the National Historic Preservation Act into law in 1966, and the National Environmental Policy Act was enacted in 1969, and the State of California followed up with the California Environmental Quality Act—all requiring that agencies of government figure out what damage their projects would do to the environment, including its cultural aspects, and try to mitigate that damage somehow—I got deeply involved in trying to make these laws work, for archaeological sites and other kinds of cultural resources. As a result, I was sort of present at the creation of CRM in the United States.

Over the years since, I've worked inside and outside government, in Washington, D.C., in California, in New York, in various other states, and in the island nations of Micronesia, occasionally doing archaeology in the field but more often negotiating agreements about how cultural resources would be managed, and writing the laws, regulations, standards, and guidelines that structure CRM. I've taken part in litigation, written books, and taught lots and lots of short courses around the country. I've been especially involved in working with Indian tribes, Micronesian and Hawaiian communities, and other indigenous, low-income, and minority groups trying to take care of their cultural resources (not just archaeological sites). One thing I've learned and come to feel strongly about through all these years of practice is that people working in CRM have to be more than just archaeologists—or historians, architectural historians, or whatever else they're trained in school to be. They have to be prepared to deal responsibly with *all* kinds of cultural resources. That's a big part of my perspective, and something I'll harp on throughout this book.

But, this book is about archaeology first and foremost.

What Archaeology Is Not

There are some widely held misconceptions about archaeology. You may not believe any of these myths, but some people do, so we'd better knock them in the head before we get into the meat of the book.

Archaeology and Dinosaurs

Archaeology is not about the study of dinosaurs or other ancient beasties—unless they're somehow associated with humans, and dinosaurs aren't. Dinosaurs died out long, long before humans came along; the two didn't coexist. Or, of course, maybe they did and nobody's discovered that fact, so if you discover it you'll become really famous, but I wouldn't plan my career around such a discovery if I were you. If you want to study dinosaurs, or other fossil animals or plants for their own sake, you don't want to do archaeology, you want to do *paleontology*—a whole different field, though paleontologists and archaeologists use a lot of similar research methods in the field and laboratory.

Treasure and Tombs

Archaeologists are not treasure hunters, or vice-versa. Of course, it's possible to find treasure while doing archaeology, or to do archaeology in connection with a search for treasure (though that's controversial; more on that later). And it's a dishonest archaeologist who tells you he or she doesn't enjoy finding something really valuable, or beautiful, or otherwise desirable. But the goal of archaeology is not to find goodies. Archaeology is about learning things, figuring things out, and the bulk of what we find and study isn't treasure. Actually, it's mostly garbage; we study what people have thrown out or otherwise left behind.

Nor is archaeology about digging into tombs. We *do* dig into tombs, and other kinds of graves, but only for a purpose. Tombs and other graves contain a great deal of information about whoever's buried there and the culture of the people who buried them, so they are of great interest to many of us. My PhD dissertation was based on the study of three cemeteries, all about 1,500 years old, in California's Sierra Nevada foothills. So, yes, we do dig tombs and other graves, but we also dig houses and backyards and public buildings and industrial sites and religious sites and—more than anything else—garbage dumps. We dig where we can get the information we want for whatever it is we're trying to learn, and in CRM we dig mostly either to help figure out how to keep things from being destroyed, or to salvage stuff that will be destroyed if we don't get it out of the way. If for either of these reasons we have to dig a

Figure 2. Up close and personal with dirt: an archaeological excavation in progress. *Photo courtesy Rob Edwards, Cabrillo College Archaeological Technology Program.*

tomb, so be it, but exhuming dead bodies isn't our reason for digging. And in the last thirty years or so, we've gotten a lot more careful about trying, if we can, *not* to dig graves; instead we try to keep them where they are. We've gotten this way not because graves aren't interesting, and full of useful information, but because people descended from those buried in them—for example Indian tribes and Native Hawaiians—have let us know in no uncertain terms that they want their ancestors left alone. We've learned—most of us, anyway—to respect both the ancestors and their descendants.

The Archaeologist as Hero

As I write this, in 2004–5, the Indiana Jones movies are getting a bit faded, and Harrison Ford has moved on to more challenging roles, but I confess to still liking the image of the archaeologist as whip-wielding adventurer. Other archaeologists protest that the image is terribly inaccurate, and of course it is. None of us is as tough as Indy, and none of us has *that* many adventures. More importantly, none of us just goes out into the sand dunes or jungles and makes great discoveries; we work long and hard at it, and go through a whole lot of drudgery on the way to finding anything exciting. Most important of all, archaeology isn't really *about* finding specific exciting things. It's about piecing together little clues to develop a general picture of something that happened in the past, to answer some general question or set of questions. And it takes a lot of very careful searching and digging and recording—taking notes, making maps and plans, drawing pictures, taking photos. Virtually none of which you ever see Indy or his ilk doing. And there are things that Indy and characters like him do—grabbing skulls, yanking stuff out of the ground—that sets us all to grinding our teeth. But still, a lot of archaeologists took to wearing fedoras in the 1980s.

Varieties of Archaeology

Depending on an archaeologist's background, training, and interests, he or she may be called a classical archaeologist, an anthropological archaeologist, a historical archaeologist, an underwater archaeologist, or some other subspecies. Rather unhelpfully to the uninitiated, all may simply call themselves "archaeologists" unless pressed to explain which kind they are.

Classical Archaeologists work with the remains of such "classical" civilizations as those of Rome and Greece, and their academic training is usually in the humanities—art history, architectural history, classical languages, history.

Anthropological Archaeologists—the most common type in the United States—come out of university programs in anthropology, the broad study of humanity. Anthropology is generally divided into four fields—sociocultural anthropology (the study of living societies and their cultures), physical anthropology (the study of the human body and its variations through time and space), linguistics (the study of language as part of culture), and archaeology (the study of culture and society in the past). Anthropological archaeologists work all over the world, but are most commonly found working with the archaeology of indigenous societies.

Historical Archaeologists study the archaeology of societies with written records (like the British colonies in North America), or to whom written records refer (like North American Indian societies with whom the British colonies interacted). They often have academic backgrounds in history, but very often are anthropological archaeologists.

Underwater Archaeologists, not surprisingly, work underwater, on shipwrecks and other submerged sites. They have various kinds of academic training, but in most cases are closely linked with historical archaeology.

In Europe and the British Commonwealth nations, many archaeologists are trained in academic programs that simply call themselves "archaeology," that aren't subsumed within fields like anthropology and classics, though particularly in nations like Canada and Australia they tend to be pretty anthropological.

To add to the confusion, there are many other specializations like industrial archaeology, commercial archaeology, aviation archaeology, and the archaeological study of particular time periods, like the Iron Age, or sets of events, like World War II. There's even a developing field of extraplanetary archaeology that concerns itself with archaeological sites on the Moon and beyond. What links all these varieties of archaeology and archaeologists together is a concern for understanding the past through the study of the stuff people have left in and on the ground.

And by the way, people spell the word in two different ways: "archaeology" and "archeology." It doesn't make a bit of difference which way you spell it, but some people do get exercised about such things.

Sites, Artifacts, and Other Esoterica

I'll try to minimize my use of esoteric terms, but there are a few I can't help using. There's a glossary at the end of the book, but I use some terms so often, and have so often found that they're confusing, that it's a good idea to say something about them before we go on.

First, there's the term *archaeological site*. Generally, this means a location studied by, or that may be studied by, archaeologists, but this gets a bit tricky. We often use the unmodified word *site* as shorthand for archaeological site. That's really not correct, of course. A site is really just a place—any place, though it's usually a place where something happened, or something is, or was, or that we distinguish in our minds somehow from other places. "The site of the World Trade Center," for example. In Chapter Two, we'll consider what makes a site archaeological.

Then there's *artifact*. An artifact is something that people in the past made—a pot, a spearpoint, a statue—that's more or less portable. Artifacts are, of course, one of the major kinds of stuff that archaeologists study. Something that *isn't* portable is often called a *feature*, or simply what it is—a floor, a wall, a pit.

When archaeologists refer to a *burial*, what they mean is a buried human body—in a grave, a tomb, some kind of burial facility (which may be only a hole in the ground or a crack in the rocks). The body is usually skeletal, though sometimes it's naturally or artificially mummified, or cremated to various degrees. Burial, of course, can also refer to the act of burying something—"the burial of Pompeii by Mount Vesuvius."

Another word we use a lot is *culture*, which has several definitions among archaeologists and anthropologists—many of them pretty complicated and full of jargon. I think a simple way to think of culture is that it's what makes us human, and what makes us think of ourselves as different kinds of humans—members of families, communities, nations, organizations. It includes ideas and beliefs in our heads and the way they're expressed in speech, songs, stories, dances, and ways of organizing ourselves to live together, find or produce food, make war, build and maintain our communities. And it includes all the physical stuff that goes along with those ideas and beliefs—artifacts, architecture, art, the computer I'm using to compose this book, the light you're reading it by, and the book itself. Archaeologists study the stuff in order to understand culture, and how it varies and changes. Culture may also be used to refer to the beliefs, ways of life, and stuff of a given group of people, in the present or the past—"Hohokam culture," "the culture of northwestern Idaho."

Finally, a word we use all the time is *data*—which simply means information. Archaeological sites contain data, and archaeologists record and work with data. The word data is the plural of the Latin *datum*, so if we're being grammatical (or some would say, old-fashioned), we say that data *are* present in a site, not that data *is* present. Picky, picky. Archaeologists find data in artifacts and relationships among artifacts and features—architecture, pits, hearths, rock piles. We find data in *stratigraphy*—how the soil of a site is layered. We find data in burials, in animal and plant remains, in the way sites are distributed over the landscape. And of course, if they're present we find data in the written word—carved into stone, pressed into clay, written on paper or papyrus—and in works of art. We can be remarkably clever in the way we ferret out information about the past. We have to be.

Now that we've introduced ourselves, the field, and some of its terminology, let's move on to the critical question of why we bother to do archaeology at all.

Chapter Two

Why Do Archaeology?

Archaeology in My Backyard

Why do archaeology? I think about this every time I work in my backyard. It's an automatic physical response, I think, because yard work involves a certain amount of digging, but it's a bit more intellectual than that. There are two things about my backyard that make me ponder why we do archaeology—and indeed, what we mean when we talk about doing archaeology.

For one thing, my house has been around for about sixty years, and had several occupants before my family and I moved in. Each set of occupants left stuff, so as I dig around planting this and removing that, building a wall and ripping out a patio, I find coins and tools and pieces of building material.[1] Evidence of past human activity, which I do *not* record, even though as an archaeologist my business is recording evidence of past human activity. Why do I not record it all, I wonder. Why, in effect, do I not regard myself as doing archaeology in my backyard?

As I work, I also think about how *my* leavings are going to look to some future archaeologist. Sometimes I do things deliberately to make them scratch their heads. "Boy, they'll wonder why this old leaf-blower is buried under this stone-walled flower bed!" Sometimes I do things to help them out—leave a coin with a date on it under a brick walk, a presidential campaign button in a wall. But more generally, I think about how everything I do leaves traces that future archaeologists will be able to interpret, if they're so inclined. They'll be able to plot my property boundaries by the rocks I've tossed out to the edges as I've reworked the soil for my wife's plantings. They'll be able to see the footings of my sheds, the brick and flagstone patios, the stone-walled raised beds that have replaced, and replicate, the ones built of now-rotted landscape timber. They'll find that Marshalltown trowel I lost, and maybe wonder if they're working at the one-time home of a fellow archaeologist. But as I think about all this, I'm also always thinking that it's pretty unlikely anyone will ever excavate my house site, because frankly, who gives a damn?

Nobody, presumably, so I don't need to treat my backyard as an archaeological site. But that raises another question.

What's an Archaeological Site?

We talk and write routinely about archaeological sites, but we're not always clear about what such a site is. Some books define the term as something like "location of past human activity," but that definition embraces every place where human beings have ever done anything at all (certainly including my backyard). As a practical matter we do not treat the entire populated world as an archaeological site. Some define it simply as a place archaeologists study, but that's a bit inaccurate, because we often call a place an archaeological site before we study it much. What we really mean by the term, I think, is "a place that an archaeologist deems worth studying."

There are two things a place must have to make it good for archaeological study. First, it has to have some sort of expression of past human activity. The remains of a building, a trash dump, a cemetery, a stretch of stone wall or earthen embankment, the vestiges of ancient agricultural fields spread over the landscape, a scatter of artifacts or other junk on the surface or in the soil. My backyard, of course, meets this criterion.

Second, the place needs to relate somehow to some kind of research that someone thinks might be useful. That's the standard that my backyard doesn't meet—yet. It might at some time in the future; someone someday might find value in studying late twentieth/early twenty-first-century backyards in the mid-Atlantic United States. But right now nobody I know of is interested in studying such backyards, so mine isn't an archaeological site, and I don't need to feel guilty about not taking notes every time I lay a flagstone or put in a water pipe.

Figure 3. Some sites are obviously important, like Pueblo Bonito in Chaco Canyon National Historical Park, New Mexico (though it *has* been excavated and cleaned up by the National Park Service. It wasn't always *this* obvious). *Photo by the author.*

Figure 4. But then there are sites like this bunch of food cans in Utah . . . *Photo courtesy SWCA Environmental Consultants.*

Figure 5. This urban archaeological excavation is exploring the backyards of the homes of nineteenth-century Irish immigrants in Washington, D.C. There are probably similar backyards throughout this part of the city. Is it an "archaeological site"? Is the whole city an archaeological site? *Photo by the author.*

A pretty slippery standard, I know, and it brings us back to the question of why we do archaeology. What makes it worth doing in, say, the buried remains of nineteenth-century Irish immigrant backyards in downtown Washington, D.C.—where I once helped design an excavation project in advance of a government building project— and not in my backyard in the Maryland suburbs?

Partly it's a matter of age. As a rough rule, the older an expression of past human activity is, the more likely we are to regard it as worthy of study.

History, Prehistory, Protohistory

Archaeologists in North America and many other parts of the world divide the past into historic and prehistoric periods. Prehistory is the time before there were contemporary written records—before people started writing about what was going on—and history is the time thereafter, up to the present. A soft, squishy period called *protohistory* is sometimes imagined as the time when some writing was going on, but not much. Since on this continent (and others, like sub-Saharan Africa) writing generally came in with European explorers and conquerors, the main periods are sometimes referred to as *precontact* and *postcontact* periods. But the Maya and other groups in what we call "Mesoamerica"—north-central Mexico down through Panama—had an elaborate writing system over a thousand years before their contact with Europeans, yet we still sometimes call the Maya prehistoric. We are usually more respectful of the indigenous writing systems of people like the Egyptians; we may refer to the Pharaohs as ancient, but not as prehistoric. Egyptian prehistory is the time before people along the Nile began to put brush to papyrus. It can be pretty confusing if you try to make fine distinctions, but if you don't get too picky the definitions are easy enough. *History* is what we've experienced in an area during the time when there's been a *lot* of contemporary documentation—lots of people writing about lots of things—particularly where the writers are members of the local culture itself. Prehistory is the time when there's little or no such documentation, and protohistory is a sort of transitional period when there's little writing about an area and what there is was written by nonnative visitors.

Most archaeologists would agree, I think, that *any place* where we find evidence of prehistoric human activity is worth some amount of study, and is hence an archaeological site. This is because such places are the only records we have of what was going on in prehistory. This is not to say that anybody necessarily wants to study every such place right now, and in fact we can and do have raging arguments about whether a given site, or a given type of site, is worth studying or preserving. But as a rough rule of thumb, if it's prehistoric it's an archaeological site. Historic sites are trickier, but again, age tends to be the prime criterion. Ancient Egyptian, Roman, or Greek sites don't lack archaeological interest just because they were built and lived in by people who had written languages, and in North America colonial-period sites are more likely to be of archaeological interest than mid-twentieth-century sites. But then there's the University of Arizona's Garbage Project, which studies modern landfills and other trash dumps, and has provided fascinating insights into twentieth-century cultural values and ways of life.[2] While nobody argues that this makes every municipal dump

Figure 6. Research interests can make a pretty nondescript site worth studying or preserving. These rings of rocks in Texas, for example, apparently represent tipi-like structures built around 1500, possibly by Plains Indian tribes that followed bison into the area during a period of climate change. *Photo by Steve Black, courtesy www.TexasBeyondHistory.net.*

into a valuable archaeological site, there's no question that useful research can be done in such places.

So—particularly where the site we're looking at reflects relatively recent human activity—the question of whether a place is in fact an archaeological site depends substantially on whether someone can make a case for learning something useful from its study.

Sites and Other Places

Incidentally, besides arguing over whether a given site is worth studying, archaeologists can also get very exercised about whether to call a place a site or something else, and about how to separate one site from another. Is an expansive system of ancient agricultural fields a site, or a bunch of sites, or what? If you have evidence of prehistoric occupation on both sides of the mouth of a river, does that make one site or two? Does the size of the river matter? What if the village is on one side, the cemetery on the other? The arguments, particularly between "lumpers" (people who'd call the two locations one site) and "splitters" (who would call them two, or maybe more) can get pretty silly at times, but more about this in Chapter Seven.

Why Study a Site?

So what makes a site—however you define it—worthy of study, and therefore archaeological? We study archaeological sites for one or more of the following reasons:

- Research: to learn something from it;
- Salvage: to save information for future use;
- Interpretation: to use sites or their contents to interpret the past for the public;
- Addressing people's interests: satisfying some expressed public (or private) desire; and
- "Because it's the law"—that is, because we think laws require it.

Let's look briefly at each of these rationales.

Research

As I said at the beginning, archaeology is a study, so it's fundamentally about doing research. Archaeologists think of themselves as researchers, trying to learn things about the past. So for most archaeologists, research is the primary reason for doing archaeology, and the primary thing that makes archaeological sites important.

We do many different kinds of research at archaeological sites, and we can have substantial arguments about whether one kind of research is better than another, or over which particular research approach should have priority in a given case. These arguments can be quite bitter, particularly because of the unique and "nonrenewable" nature of archaeological resources (see Chapter Three for more on this topic). When we dig up an archaeological site we destroy it, and we lose information. No matter how carefully we keep records, we always miss things. So if you and I are both interested in a site for different research reasons, and I dig it up, there's a good chance I'll destroy information that's important to you. That—for you, at least—is likely to be a problem.

Sometimes our research is designed to fill in gaps in the historical record, or flesh it out. For example, I've been involved for over fifteen years with The International Group for Historic Aircraft Recovery (TIGHAR) in an attempt to ascertain what happened to aviation pioneer Amelia Earhart when she disappeared over the Pacific in 1937.[3] When I was a student archaeologist at what's now San Francisco State University, back in the 1960s, I worked on projects trying to identify where the British explorer Francis (later Sir Francis) Drake landed on the California coast in 1579.[4]

A wonderful example of filling out the historical record is the work done by Wolfgang Schluter and his colleagues on the Battle of the Teutoburg Forest in Germany, where German warriors wiped out three complete Roman Legions in A.D. 09, halting the expansion of the Roman Empire at the Rhine River and literally changing the course of world history.[5] Only fragmentary accounts of the battle can be found in surviving Roman texts, and there is no written account of it at all from the German perspective, but archaeology—both at the battle site and in contemporary residential and burial sites—has provided a richly detailed picture of this pivotal event.

Much archaeological research is more or less descriptive and reconstructive, aimed at recreating a general picture of what happened during some ancient period in some part of the world. Much, if not most, of what we know about the Maya, the Inca, and other ancient civilizations of the Americas, as well as the ancient Egyptians, Babylonians, Sumerians, Hittites, Celts, Harappans, Huns, Mongols, Chinese, Kikiyu—you name them—is derived from reconstructive archaeological research. In North America, a vast amount of research has been devoted just to trying to figure out what happened during prehistory in different areas—the Mississippi River basin, the Great Basin, the Southwest. This sort of research is sometimes called *culture history*. Most reconstructive research is focused on particular more or less well-defined cultural groups, like the Hohokam and Anasazi of the American Southwest, or the Mississippian cultures in the Southeast. These are all names—and groups—made up by archaeologists, but they're thought to represent real cultural entities of some kind, and archaeologists seek to reconstruct how they developed and changed through time. A lot of such research also focuses on the question of when and how human beings first came to North America, and there are many arguments between proponents of—for example—an initial immigration from Siberia down between the glaciers around 15,000 years ago and seagoing passage around the North Atlantic a good deal earlier. I should mention that in the eyes of many Native Americans this whole line of research is irrelevant and rather insulting; they've learned from their traditions that they've been here forever, or came here from another world. Considerate archaeologists respect this belief as one version of reality, but recognize that in other versions the ancestors of today's tribes, like the rest of us, came originally out of Africa and must have gotten from there to here somehow.

In my own career, back in the 1970s when I started working in the islands of Micronesia we knew almost nothing about the prehistory of the place, and much of our research was directed simply at exploring the sites we found in Yap, Chuuk, Pohnpei, and other island groups to see what they could tell us. Because of the times in which we were working, however, many of us weren't very satisfied with a purely reconstructive approach.

This is because, in the 1960s, a group of archaeologists mostly clustered around Louis Binford and the University of Chicago developed something that was then called *New Archaeology*. New Archaeology challenged us to be more explicitly scientific and anthropological about the research we did. We shouldn't just try to reconstruct the past, Binford and his colleagues argued; we should try to formulate and answer serious questions about the human condition and the processes by which that condition—human culture—develops and changes. Why, for example, do we even *have* complex cultures—civilizations? Why weren't our ancestors satisfied to roam the earth hunting and gathering in small, egalitarian groups? Why do we make war, and what alternatives are there to doing so? What are the different ways that human cultures respond to environmental or economic stress? What causes a complex culture to collapse? Because of this concern for cultural processes, the New Archaeologists were also called *processualists*. And they were sometimes called *positivists* because they believed that a more or less definite set of facts—truth, if you will—about the past could be teased out of the data they collected, though the same thing could be said about archaeologists who do culture history.[6]

The other thing the New Archaeologists argued for was that our research ought to be hypothetico-deductive. We should, they said, formulate hypotheses—a fancy word for educated guesses—about the answers to our research questions through deduction, which means reasoning from general principles. We should then conduct our research in such a way as to test these hypotheses. The New Archaeologists wanted to make archaeological practice much more like what chemists and physicists do. Albert Einstein hypothesized that massive things like stars distort space-time. Based on Einstein's equations, Joseph Lense and Hans Thirring then showed that such a distortion might be observable in effects on small orbiting bodies. Only recently have instruments been precise enough to measure such effects on satellites, confirming the hypothesis. The New Archaeologists said that archaeology could do the same kind of thing—though in a rather cruder way. We could, for example, develop hypotheses about why some groups of people in the past have developed complex forms of government—kings and aristocrats lording it over commoners—and others have not, and then test these hypotheses through the study of archaeological data.

I was particularly taken by the New Archaeology, and in developing and promoting research in Micronesia tried very hard to make it as hypothetico-deductive as possible. Some of the cultures of Micronesia were traditionally very complex and hierarchical, with powerful chiefly groups that controlled the labor of lower classes; they'd built and maintained big stone cities like Nan Madol on the island of Pohnpei, now a complex of impressive ruins on the island's shore and reef. Other groups, for example those of Chuuk where my wife and I did a lot of research, had never developed such centralized organization. We asked ourselves why this was so—as a small version of the question: "why do human beings develop complex forms of social organization?" Then we tried to formulate alternative answers, based on principles derived from ecology, sociology, and other disciplines, and to test them.[7]

We were not notably successful, and neither were others who made such attempts in different parts of the world. As a result, a lot of archaeologists—maybe most, maybe in a way all—fell away from "New Archaeology" and went off in a variety of postprocessual directions. These in turn reflect a broader trend in recent scholarship often referred to as *postmodernism* or *postpositivism*. Postpositivists reject the idea that there's absolute truth to be found through research, and define science as a sort of creative dialogue between researcher and data. Some postmodern archaeologists ground their theory in literary criticism, and hold that our interpretations of what we dig up are simply stories we tell about the past, which are more or less plausible and useful in understanding the human condition.[8] They may be right (if it's possible to say that anything's right in the absence of truth), but I get a bit uncomfortable with archaeological studies that blur the distinctions between reporting what's observed in and on the ground and telling a story to account for the observations. I suppose I'm still a New Archaeologist, albeit a pretty old one. One of the great contributions of postmodern archaeology, though (and more broadly, postmodern anthropology), has been to tell stories about the past from hitherto neglected perspectives. For example, there's widespread interest in "engendered" archaeology, which in essence means better understanding the roles of women in the workings and transformations of culture.

Sometimes an archaeologist will say that his or her research is simply descriptive, just aimed at describing what's in the ground in order to record it for future reference. This most often is done in connection with *salvage* or *rescue archaeology* (see below). Most archaeologists don't say this, though, even if they believe it, because it's regarded as a bit lazy ("You mean you can't think of *any* research questions to ask about this site?"). I think most of us would also say—and some of us have said it, quite vehemently—that you can never just objectively describe an archaeological site in all its complexity. The description of an archaeological site and its contents is always a dynamic interaction between the site and the person doing the description; we're always selecting what we record and collect. We don't record the precise location, specific gravity, and chemistry of every molecule of soil; we don't collect every pebble. What we're interested in—what we think is important—always influences the way we excavate and document a site, and our research interests define what we think is interesting and important. So whatever our research interests are, it's an important part of good practice to make them as explicit as possible, and we ought to be able to explain and defend them.

Salvage

A lot of archaeologists don't like to use the word salvage for what they do. It summons up images of the "bad old days" of the 1950s and '60s, when we scrabbled to save what we could in advance of the bulldozer blade, with little time and less money, and no opportunity whatever to influence planning in such a way as to actually save sites intact. But like it or not, we often wind up excavating sites for purposes of salvage—or rescue, as it tends to be called in many British Commonwealth countries and elsewhere. We may have more money than we used to, and we may have more time, but we're still digging primarily because the site we're interested in is going to be destroyed.

Salvage or rescue archaeology is done under two circumstances: at the end of a planning process, and as the result of a discovery.

In most cases we've gone through the planning, studies, and consultations that are fundamental to the practice of cultural resource management (see Chapter Five), and at the end of the day, it's decided that a site has to go, to make way for a highway or an airport, a sewage treatment plant, or a levee. Or the whole site may not go; it may be necessary only to dig a pipeline trench through it, or carve off a corner of it to widen the highway. In these cases an excavation project is planned and carried out, usually funded by whoever will benefit from the project that's messing up the site. These excavation projects are usually pretty orderly affairs, and although we have great arguments over how well a given project is done, they can, if things go well, be made into excellent research projects. We develop research designs, often formulating hypotheses derived from general theory or at least dealing with research topics that people think are important, and then do fieldwork that's designed to test the hypotheses and address the topics. We usually have (more or less) enough time to do the work in an organized way, and analyze the results.

We also do archaeology as part of the planning process *before* getting to the decision to excavate and sacrifice a site. That is, we do archaeological surveys and test excavations in order to determine what impacts a project will have, or what sites exist on a piece of land that somebody needs to manage. This work, too, is usually done in a reasonably leisurely, orderly way that makes it possible to do good research—though of course it doesn't always work that way, and there are plenty of horror stories about archaeologists racing the bulldozers.

We don't always find everything in the course of planning, and that leads to the second circumstance under which we do archaeology for purposes of rescue or salvage. For one reason or another, a site isn't found during planning, pops up during construction, and whoever's doing the construction is observant enough to notice it and honorable enough to hold off destroying it until archaeologists can salvage whatever they can. Or maybe it's found during planning, but its extent, complexity, or importance isn't realized until whatever is going to destroy it is underway. The African Burial Ground in New York City, for example—a colonial-era burial place for enslaved Africans—was identified from an old map during planning for a federal office building, but its significance wasn't really understood until archaeological testing began to reveal lots and lots of skeletons in the ground, by which time construction was already underway on the site. The result was a horribly controversial situation in which construction had to be stopped, the project redesigned, things worked out (more or less) with a very aggrieved African-American population, and a massive archaeological excavation carried out through the winter—not the time you want to be doing archaeology in New York. It cost tens of millions of dollars, and rubbed the scabs off emotional wounds dating back to the days of slavery that aren't yet really healed.[9] Nearby, and as part of the same overall construction project, the core of Five Points—the notorious eighteenth-to-nineteenth-century slum known to moviegoers from Martin Scorsese's *Gangs of New York*—was excavated in an orderly way as the outcome of thoughtful planning, because *its* significance was understood and allowed for in project planning.[10]

Interpretation

We often do archaeology as part of public interpretation—that is, to prepare a site for use in such interpretation, or to gather data for this purpose. That's seldom the only purpose; we're usually also trying to find out something about the site (research) or taking care of something that's in danger (salvage or rescue), but interpretation is often an important motivator. The first professional dig I worked on—the archaeologist in charge, A. E. Treganza of San Francisco State College (later my undergraduate mentor), told his crew chief that if that skinny kid was going to hang around gawking, he might as well be put to work—was such a project, at the Petaluma Adobe in California.[11] The Adobe—a big mud-brick fort built in the 1830s–1840s at the direction of Mexican pioneer Mariano Vallejo—had recently (in the late 1950s) been acquired by the State. The north half of it still stood; the south half had collapsed and melted away. Treganza's job was to excavate enough of the foundations to give the State a basis for deciding whether and how to reconstruct it, and to see if he could find evidence of what the collapsed rooms had been used for. In the end, the decision was made not to reconstruct the lost part of the building, but the results of the dig, and subsequent research, contributed to interpretation of the site. Virtually any interpreted historic site you visit—Colonial Williamsburg, Mesa Verde, Moundville, Stonehenge—has experienced this kind of excavation, though the less is known about the site from other sources, the more the archaeology there has been justified as research rather than simply as a way to guide interpretation.

People's Interests

We sometimes do archaeology simply because someone wants it done, though the motivation is usually a lot more complex than that sounds, and usually it's only one of several reasons for doing the work. The African Burial Ground in New York is an example. Excavation of the ABG was entirely justified by the need to rescue the hundreds of graves that would otherwise have been destroyed by construction, and the research being done on the remains is fascinating. It's revealing a great deal about what it was like to be an enslaved African in New York in the seventeenth and eighteenth centuries (pretty grim), and it may make it possible to reconstruct linkages between families in the United States and their ancestral communities in Africa. But there's no question that the excavation would not have been as extensive or complete as it was if it weren't for the very forcefully expressed desires of the African-American community in New York and elsewhere. The people wanted their ancestors taken care of, and they weren't about to take no for an answer.

A quite different example is the case of the British warship *Sussex*, which went down in the Straits of Gibraltar in 1694. The *Sussex* was carrying a substantial cargo of coinage—intended as payment to the Duke of Savoy to keep him allied with the British against the French—which Her Majesty's Government would like to get back. The marine exploration company Odyssey, out of Tampa, Florida, believes it's found the wreck of the *Sussex* and wants to salvage it. Odyssey naturally has economic motivations—a share in the treasure, as well as the benefits to be obtained from exhibiting and interpreting the ship and its cargo. Odyssey and Her Majesty's Government have every intention of doing excellent archaeological research on the wreck, and have engaged a Sussex Archaeological Executive—a sort of quality-control oversight group of archaeologists on which I'm privileged to serve—to help make sure that's what's done, but there's no question that the work wouldn't be done if it weren't for the economic interests of the two sponsoring parties.[12]

"Because it's the law"

Finally, we sometimes do archaeology because we understand that we're legally required to do it. Usually this justification arises in connection with some kind of planning—somebody is proposing to put in a highway or a shopping mall, an archaeological site is in the way, and it's excavated because the project proponent understands or is advised that excavation is required by law. "The law," it's thought, protects the precious remains of the past, at least to the extent that it requires careful excavation before allowing archaeological sites to be destroyed.

In point of fact, the law is seldom so straightforward. There are lots of national, state and provincial, Indian tribal, and local laws and regulations requiring that some kind of attention be paid to archaeological sites, but there's no universally applicable legal requirement that they be excavated before something destroys them. The federal laws in the United States apply only to projects in which there's some kind of federal agency involvement—federal funds, for example, or a federal license, or the use of federal land. State and local laws vary widely in their requirements; some apply pretty specific requirements to a wide range of state and locally regulated or funded projects, while others don't. Many privately funded projects on private land are subject to no archaeological requirements at all. In other countries—throughout Latin America, for example—archaeological sites or at least the stuff they contain are regarded in law as government property, by virtue of being parts of the national patrimony, but that doesn't mean that the government systematically imposes requirements on property owners and developers; more often than not, it's pretty easy to get away with archaeological site destruction if one wants to.

Moreover, even where there *are* relevant laws, and they *are* enforced, they don't usually (or ever, in my experience) require excavation per se. They require that steps be taken to protect sites and/or their contents, or manage them somehow, or just consider them in planning, but they don't specifically say you've got to hire archaeologists to excavate them. There are often very good alternatives to excavation, like redesigning a project to leave a site protected somehow, maybe covered with fill or in a landscaped area.

But I still hear people say, from time to time, that "the law requires" excavation of every significant site that's threatened by construction or changing land use. This is plain nonsense.

Where some sort of protective law applies, what it *does* require is planning, consideration, consultation with concerned parties, and some kind of management. In other words, as we'll see, cultural resource management. And cultural resource management is not just archaeology.

Chapter Three

Principles and Practice

In this chapter, I want to explore some basic principles and how they structure the ways we do archaeology. These aren't arranged in any particular order, because I can't think of an ordering scheme that makes much sense. However, I'll begin with one of the key principles of cultural resource management—that we need to recognize and respect multiple interests in cultural resources like archaeological sites and artifacts.

Archaeological and Other Interests in the Past

An archaeologist is interested in stuff from the past because he or she wants to learn something from it. Exactly what it is we want to learn may be very general and unspecific: "I wonder what life was really like in Five Points?" Or it may have a much more specific focus: "What caused the Anasazi to abandon the Chaco Canyon area in the twelfth century A.D.?" But whatever it is, our basic interest is in information. If you're interested in stuff from the past for some other reason, you may be able to *do* archaeology, but you're not really an archaeologist.

But there are other, very legitimate interests in the past that an archaeologist needs to understand and respect. A community that regards itself as descended from the ancient people of an area, or as responsible for taking care of the ancient ones' places and things, probably doesn't give a fig for the information that those places and things contain, but its people are very concerned about the places and things themselves. Indian tribes and other indigenous groups are the obvious examples.

Figure 7. This is a traditional lodge on the Klamath River in California, used in a complex series of rituals by the Karuk Tribe for purposes of renewing the world and all that's in it. A very, very spiritually powerful, sacred place to the Karuk, but if the lodge were gone, it would look to an archaeologist like a good site to excavate. We have to be very careful to remember that other people view the places we dig, and our digging itself, in ways that are very different from the way we may view them. *Photo by the author, with tribal permission.*

Notice that my example was a community that *regards itself* as descended from ancient residents, or *regards itself* as responsible for their places and things. Since concern about places and things exists in people's heads and hearts, it doesn't matter a bit whether you or I or the Supreme Court think they're *really* descended from the ancient folks, or *really* have some sort of caretaking responsibility. If they believe it, they believe it, and they have an interest that needs to be respected. It may not in the end determine what happens to a place or thing, but it's a legitimate concern and can't be disregarded. If a tribe says its ancestors built the pueblos up in the canyon, that's what it believes, and it's irrelevant that you, the archaeologist, "know" based on years of research that they really migrated into the area 500 years after the pueblos were built.

Another legitimate interest that archaeologists often have trouble understanding is really a whole package of cultural and aesthetic interests. People may like things from the past because they're beautiful, or because they make them feel grounded, or linked to history, connected to a place, or inspired somehow. They may believe them to be imbued with spiritual power—consider the Temple Mount in Jerusalem, obviously an archaeological site but to devout Jews, Muslims, and Christians, much more than that.

A great deal of cultural resource management (CRM) is based on such interests—on how people *feel* about places and things. We preserve Martin Luther King Jr.'s birthplace in the Sweet Auburn District of Atlanta, Georgia, not because the old house can teach us anything we don't already know about Dr. King, but because of the respect we have for him and the inspiration his life and works have given so many people. We preserve the Vieux Carre Historic District in New Orleans (the French Quarter) not because it teaches us about the Big Easy but because it evokes a sense of time and place, exudes an ambience, that's different from what's evoked by, say, a strip mall in the suburbs. The Lakota treasure the Black Hills of South Dakota and Wyoming because they are a spiritual place, intimately tied up in Lakota origins, traditions, and religious beliefs. The displaced residents of the area they call "Between the Rivers" in western Kentucky fight to participate in its management—it's now the Land Between the Lakes National Recreation Area—because it's the place with which they feel historically and culturally associated, the place that defines their identity. All these interests can be very powerful. Sometimes they coincide with an archaeologist's interests in information, and sometimes they conflict.

Then there are educational interests—not so much in learning new things from sites and their contents, but in using archaeological data to teach things to others. Obviously there is a large and very important role for archaeology to play in public education, and the interests of educators in using the stuff we excavate, the sites we study, are interests archaeologists ought to respect and seek to advance. But they can sometimes conflict with our interests, in small ways and large. It takes time away from the excavations to go talk to local school kids. Using a site to educate people about the Archaic period may require us to remove deposits of stuff from later periods that lie on top of the Archaic stuff. Usually not irresoluble conflicts, but they can exist and need to be resolved.

Another interest in the past is economic. Whether we like it or not, artifacts like pots, baskets, statuary, and the like can be worth money—sometimes lots of money—and as a result, people want to buy and sell them. Archaeologists commonly express shock and revulsion at this, because we value artifacts for the information that they—and the relationships between them as they lie in the ground— can give us, and we assume that such information will be lost if things are dug up for and trafficked in the marketplace.

But economic value is a fact of life. Where something is worth money, it's naïve not to take this into account. And it's important to recognize that unless it's against the law, society says it's OK for people to buy and sell the stuff. It certainly *is* against the law to buy and sell some kinds of archaeological material—notably in the United States, material that comes from federal land—but a great deal of commerce in artifacts is perfectly legal. Archaeologists don't have to approve of, or cooperate with, people who buy and sell artifacts; but on the other hand, we won't go to jail if we do, pro- vided *they're* not breaking any laws. Many archaeological organizations, however, forbid their members from cooperating with artifact collectors or dealers, and cancel their memberships or oth- erwise censure them if they do. That's a fact of life, too; I think it's rather silly, but it's the way these organizations have chosen to do business. It gives them the comfort of occupying, in their eyes, the moral high ground; whether it does anything to discourage com- mercial traffic in artifacts is something else again.

I think that when we try to deny the legitimacy of a collector's fascination with artifacts, we simply stick our heads in the sand; we would do better to acknowledge their interests and see what can be done to find common ground. But be careful about following my advice—it can get you in trouble with virtually every organized archaeological group in the world.

My overall point here is simply that archaeological interests aren't the only interests in the stuff left to us from the past, and we always have to be aware of, and in various ways responsive to, other interests. In my own practice, I try to accommodate and cooperate with other interests as much as I possibly, ethically can. I think that's good practice, especially for a cultural resource manager, and I recommend it.

Data versus Stuff

Turning to a principle that's more specific to archaeology—it's fundamental that while we work with *stuff*, what we're interested in are *data*. We aren't concerned about the artifacts as *artifacts*, we're concerned about what they can teach us.

This is reflected in practice by the fact that in the field and laboratory we record all kinds of things about whatever it is we collect, and what we collect is a lot more than artifacts. Some of the things we record and collect besides artifacts include:

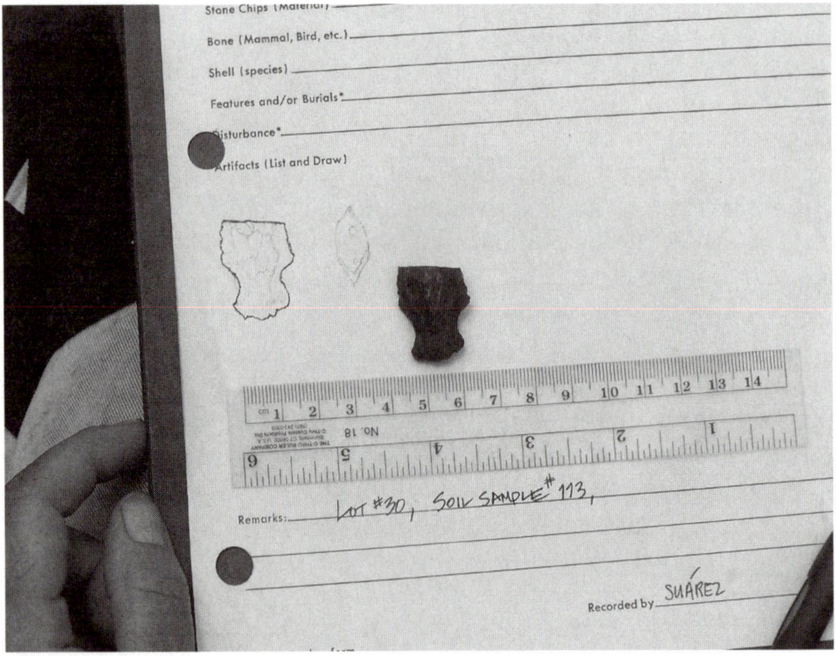

Figure 8. Data from stuff. Recording information on an artifact in the field: what is it, where did it come from? *Photo courtesy Rob Edwards, Cabrillo College Archaeological Technology Program.*

Ecofacts. This esoteric term refers to stuff that comes from the natural environment but may be found in an archaeological site (or sometimes elsewhere) and that is useful in archaeological research. Examples include animal bones, shells, teeth, feathers, and feces; plant remains, and pollen.

Architecture. If the site or area contains standing structures or the remains of standing structures associated with whatever we're studying, we'll record them, usually in considerable detail.

Features. This term is generally used to refer to some nonportable or not-very-portable thing in a site that we record because we think it may mean something. A feature may be architectural—a housepit, a foundation, a wall—or it may be something else—a storage pit, a firepit, a ditch, a pile of rocks. We may not know exactly what it is, or what it means. Maybe it's a patch of earth that's a different color than the ground around it, or that has a different texture or consistency. We may have no idea why it's like that, but we'll record it as a feature, take notes on it, take samples from it, and try to figure out what it is.

Graves and human remains. Although we're not the tomb raiders some popular media make us out to be, graves and their contents—and human remains even if they're not in graves—are important objects of archaeological study. Besides what we can learn from the artifacts that may be in them—and the fact that some artifacts may occur in graves but nowhere else, or be found other places but never in graves—the shape, size, and construction of the grave facility itself—the grave shaft, the tomb, or whatever—can give us useful information. And the human skeleton is full of information, about the age, sex, health, and even life activities of the person whose skeleton it is, and through analysis of DNA that can be extracted from bones and teeth, about the relationships between a given skeleton and other people, living and dead.

Stratigraphic relationships. What kind of soil layers are we dealing with, and more generally, how do things in the soil lie in vertical relationship with one another? As a general rule (though there are lots of exceptions) stuff that's deep in the ground is older than stuff

Figure 9. Simple stratigraphy in a California coastal site. The dark, organic soil full of shellfish remains is referred to as *midden*, which basically means decayed trash. *Photo courtesy Rob Edwards, Cabrillo College Archaeological Technology Program.*

that's shallow, particularly if the shallow stuff is in a layer of soil (a *stratum*) that's clearly different from the layer the deep stuff is in. So we record stratigraphic data with as much precision as we can.

Horizontal relationships. We're also concerned about how stuff of all kinds relates to other stuff in horizontal space. This may be big horizontal space—how sites relate to geographic features in a whole river valley or stretch of coastline or mountain range—or it may be small-scale horizontal space within a site or small area. We're concerned about horizontal relationships for the same reason a crime scene investigator is—we're trying to reconstruct what happened in this piece of space, and the relationships among things will help us do it. If the gun is in the hand of the body on the floor with a bullet hole in its head, maybe it's evidence of suicide; if there's no

Figure 10. An extreme example of stratigraphy. Arenosa Shelter at Amistead Reservoir, Texas. *Photo courtesy www.TexasBeyondHistory.net, Texas Archaeological Research Laboratory, University of Texas at Austin.*

gun around but the bullet hole's there, maybe it's murder. In the same way, if bone needles are found near the fire pit, maybe it means that people used to sew by the fire at night or when it wasn't very nice outside; if needles are never found by the fire but do turn up on the creek bank 20 meters away, that probably means they sewed during the daytime when it wasn't raining.

Horizontal stratigraphy. A sort of confusing term that refers to how stuff can get sorted horizontally over the land surface through time. Maybe 2,000 years ago people live on a site for a while and then move away. Fifteen hundred years ago people return to the site—maybe the descendants of those who lived there before, maybe somebody else—but they don't set up shop on exactly the same place as people did before; they're a bit off to one side. The stuff that they leave may overlap or mix with the stuff left by the earlier people, or maybe it doesn't. When an archaeologist comes along and studies the site, he or she is going to need to sort out the older stuff from the younger, but there may be no vertical difference between them—they're all on more or less the same horizontal plane or slope. The horizontal differences between the older and younger deposits are what we're talking about when we refer to horizontal stratigraphy.

Environmental data. We're usually very interested in the natural environment within which a site lies. Is it on a stream? Next to a spring? On a coast? At the junction of woodland and meadow? At a boundary between soil types? Knowing about the environment can help us understand what a site was used for, what people did there. Since we're concerned about what happened in the past, we record not only contemporary environmental data but *paleoenvironmental* data—information indicating what the environment used to be like in the past.

When it comes to artifacts themselves, it's also the data we're concerned about, so in looking at a beautiful pot—though we're not immune to its beauty—we're likely to be especially interested in the technology used to shape it—was it coiled, thrown on a wheel, or what?—and how its decoration compares with the decoration on other pots, or even in the food residue stuck on the inside. We'll record all these data, along with data on how the stone spearpoints were chipped, how the metal artifacts (if there are any) were made, and so on, and it's these data we'll use in our analysis. The artifacts themselves, in theory at least, aren't important to us; what's important is the information we can glean from them.

The Importance of Context

Although artifacts, ecofacts, burials, and features themselves contain information, or can be studied to derive information, it's often the relationships among things that really tell the story. These relationships—including vertical and horizontal stratigraphy and the other horizontal relationships mentioned above—are collectively referred to as *context*, and it's usually a major preoccupation on any archaeological project to record it.

The importance of context is pretty obvious when you think about it. If we don't know which artifacts are higher than which others in a given set of soil layers (that is, in the vertical

Figure 11. Why archaeologists hate pothunters. Whoever collected these potsherds at Chaco Canyon National Historical Park and left them on a rock made it impossible for archaeologists to learn anything from their original context. *Photo by the author.*

stratigraphy), we're missing an important indicator of their relative ages. If we haven't recorded whether the bone needles came from next to the fire pit or down by the creek, we're missing a clue about where and at what time of day sewing went on—which in turn might be useful in sorting out things like the season at which the site was occupied or the way the sexes related to one another.

It's because of the importance of context that archaeologists almost always carefully map the sites they dig and the areas they survey. And when we dig, we typically lay out some kind of mapped and controlled area or areas within which the digging takes place. If there's nothing about the site that suggests we ought to do otherwise—like an obvious piece of architecture to explore—we'll probably overlay the site with some kind of grid system, perhaps of one-meter or two-meter squares, and then excavate blocks or trenches made up of these squares, or a lot of squares scattered all over the site, selected according to some kind of system we think will give us a representative sample of the whole site.

Within whatever kinds of units we excavate, we'll keep careful track of vertical context, keeping each observable soil level separate from each other, and collecting stuff with reference to the level it came from. If the levels are very thick, or not distinguishable from one another, we may use arbitrary measured levels, for example, levels 10 centimeters thick. (More on all this in Chapter Four.) The point is that when we're done, we want to be able to reconstruct as precisely as possible where each thing we recorded—artifact, feature, ecofact, soil sample—was when we found it.

The importance of context is also one of the major reasons that archaeologists get so upset with pothunters. If somebody digs up a pot from a site we want to study, what's bothersome is not only that the pot is gone but that he or she has messed up the context the pot was in—disrupted the soil strata, disturbed the patterns of artifacts and ecofacts in the ground. He or she has deprived us of not only the ability to study the pot, but also the ability to understand a whole piece of the site—maybe the whole site, if it's taken a lot of digging to find the pot. We also lose data about the artifacts themselves. If the pothunter repents and brings the pot in to a museum, we'll probably be able to tell by looking at it what kind of pot it is, and perhaps how old it is, but there will be a great deal we can't learn without studying its context in the ground—which of course has been lost to us. Was it in a house? What kind of house? What else was around it? Grinding tools and storage pits, suggesting that it might have been used in food storage or preparation? Broken drinking vessels, suggesting it might have been used in some celebratory bacchanalia? What was in it that's been cleaned out to make it acceptable to the pothunter's finicky housekeeping husband? Burned beans? The ashes of some cremated dead guy? Wine residue? These kinds of data bring the artifact to life, and let us make sense of it as part of the culture that produced and used it. Without them, it's just a pretty pot.

Hypotheses and Tests

If the New Archaeology of the 1960s and '70s did nothing else for us, it taught many of us the utility of generating and testing hypotheses. Hypotheses help us stay focused, and rationalize the decisions we make about where to survey, where to dig, what to record, what to keep, what to throw away. A hypothesis is basically a guess about something, but it's based on some kind of evidence or deductive logic—that is, reasoning based on a general principle. When you say, "I think I left my car keys in the kitchen because I had them in my hand when I brought in the groceries," you're formulating a hypothesis ("The keys are in the kitchen") based on data ("I remember having the keys when I carried the groceries into the kitchen") and deductive logic ("As a general principle, it's more likely that I left them someplace I *was*, rather than someplace I *wasn't*").

In our work on the Amelia Earhart project, we hypothesize that the lost flyers (Earhart and her navigator, Fred Noonan) landed and died on the island of Nikumaroro. We formulated this hypothesis initially because the last course they were known to be flying would have taken them to this island, and because radio messages received after they disappeared, initially thought to have come from their plane and never really explained away, could have been transmitted by Earhart only if the plane were on land somewhere and could run an engine to generate electricity. As we've gone along we've generated subhypotheses, like: "They landed in the clearing alongside Baureke Passage and the plane was then washed by storms into the lagoon"—and tested these with specific kinds of fieldwork on land and underwater.

That's the beauty of hypotheses—they can be tested. You can test the hypothesis that you left your car keys in the kitchen by going into the kitchen and looking. That's a lot more efficient than just wandering around the house hoping your keys will show up. It's the same way in archaeology. A hypothesis gives structure and efficiency to a piece of archaeological research. Our fieldwork along Baureke Passage and in the part of the lagoon where we thought the plane might have gone didn't support our subhypothesis, so we discarded it and developed another based on better data. Overall, though, our research on Nikumaroro and other islands *has* supported the general hypothesis that Earhart landed and died there, though it hasn't yet produced ironclad proof. Structuring our research to test the "Nikumaroro Hypothesis" has given us a basis for figuring out what to do, what not to do, how to budget our limited time and money. It's been a lot more efficient than just wandering from island to island or sweeping the sea looking for evidence of Earhart and her plane.

Archaeology as a Box of Tools

I think it's useful to think of archaeology not as a science or discipline in its own right, but as a box of tools that we use to investigate hypotheses derived from other disciplines, or simply from life. Or you can think of archaeology as a craft, or an art form, that we employ in trying to examine questions asked by such other disciplines. The box of tools notion is a useful one because it reminds us of our reliance on other disciplines, and hence our need to know something about them. Hypotheses about the rise and fall of complex cultures, or the development of agriculture, or the cultural effects of environmental change aren't based on archaeological theory; they come from anthropology, ecology, and sociology. In studying the Earhart disappearance we're addressing a question that intrigues historians (and the general public), and the project involves not only archaeologists but oceanographers, forensic anthropologists, historians, meteorologists, ecologists, geologists, biologists, radio scientists, and experts in aeronautics and aviation technology.

Figures 12 & 13. Using the most appropriate tool. We used a huge tracked "Gradall" to expose pit features on Tinian Island in the Commonwealth of the Northern Mariana Islands. Then students from the University of Guam used hand tools to expose each pit's details so they could record them. *Photos by the author and Dr. Hiro Kuroshina, University of Guam.*

It's also helpful because it reminds us to be flexible. There's no set, rote way to do archaeology, any more than there is to do carpentry or plumbing. You don't cut a piece of wood with a screwdriver; you go for a saw or a knife, a plane or a router, depending on what kind of cutting you want to do—and, of course, on what tools you have in your box. In the same way, the popular image of the archaeologist digging with a trowel and a camel's hair brush is accurate in some cases, grossly not so in others. There's no standard, set way to do archaeology, particularly archaeological fieldwork. Which brings us to another principle.

Use the Crudest Tool That Does the Job

The late Jesse Jennings of the University of Utah, a major figure in the development of archaeology in the western United States, put it this way:

> In my attempts to teach field procedures I constantly enjoin students to always "use the coarsest tool which will do the work—i.e. recover the data." A shovel can be as useful as a trowel, a road patrol or scraper as useful as a shovel, or a dragline as useful as a pick, in the hands of an investigator who is free of ritual compulsiveness.[1]

In other words, don't waste time trying to clear a collapsed pueblo using a camel's hair paintbrush, unless there's something about this particular pueblo, or the particular information you're trying to extract from it, that demands it. Use a whisk broom, or a trowel, or a shovel, or a backhoe—whatever's in your box of tools that gets you the information you need in the most efficient manner.

Beginners in archaeology often have trouble with this principle, because they don't quite know which tool is the most appropriate to the circumstances, and because their (quite proper) respect for the site they're digging makes them hypercareful. That's perfectly understandable, but what's sad is when doing things in a particular, hypercautious way becomes ingrained as an archaeologist matures in the field, and turns into a sort of ethic. "We always dig one-by-one-meter units." "We always excavate natural levels." "We always screen all the dirt." This is a particular problem in CRM-related archaeology, where we need to maintain flexibility in order to relate efficiently to situations beyond our control. I once had to excavate three cemeteries in a very short time before they were scheduled to be rooted out to make way for a dam. I used two bulldozers—not to dig the graves themselves, of course, but to remove the *overburden*—the soil overlying the graves—and to establish the edges of the cemeteries, which we then dug (very rapidly) by hand. It was the only way to get the information my research demanded (data on how the cemeteries were organized and on the individuals buried there) in the time available before the sites and burials were ground into oblivion. But some of my colleagues were so appalled by my choice of tools that I started calling the two bulldozers Trowel and Brush.

Efficiency is Balanced With Responsibility

We have the responsibility—notably to those who finance our work—to do our archaeology as efficiently as we can. At the same time, we have to balance efficiency against a variety of other responsibilities, many of which have nothing much to do with archaeology but often involve those other interests with which I began this discussion of principles.

We're responsible as archaeologists for the integrity of the data we extract from the ground and translate into other forms. That's what archaeologists do, really—we get data out of the ground, or out of the environment, and translate it into books and monographs and research articles in journals. So one of our most basic responsibilities is to shepherd those data from the ground to the page. A lot of our techniques and methods are designed to do this—our mapping, our use of controlled excavation units, the notes we take, the photographs, the numbers we put on artifacts in the lab and storage facility. (We'll discuss all this in Chapter Four.) Even when we're under great duress, we need to figure out ways to discharge this responsibility. When I was an undergraduate at San Francisco State University back in the '60s, my friends and I developed a fast way to record a site's features during their destruction by road construction, using tape recorders and a surveyor's transit. We adapted this method to several other site-destruction situations, collecting a lot of data that would otherwise have been lost. These days, of course, we have far better technology to employ, like global positioning system (GPS) trackers and digital videocameras, but I'm still rather proud of what we developed back then. We got the data that we could get, in the most efficient way we could. If we'd been hung up on having to employ standard archaeological methods like laying out excavation units and taking notes on paper, the data would have been lost. I felt that what we did was an exercise in responsibility.

But we have other responsibilities, too, and the examples I've just described highlight them both.

In my cemetery excavation I obviously dealt with a lot of dead people—almost five hundred in all. There were burials in the site we recorded with the tape recorders, too, and we had to photograph them, describe them on tape, and then quickly root out the bones, get them into bags, and get them off the site before the next pass of the bulldozer. In those days we didn't think much about this; graves were simply another—very rich—source of data that we recorded and extracted. The bones went into boxes and drawers back at the laboratory, were analyzed to extract more data, and then were simply kept. Or, in some very unfortunate cases, thrown away or lost. But the '60s were also the years of not only Black Power—Martin Luther King Jr., Malcolm X, the marches on Selma and Washington—but Red Power. There was the American Indian Movement, occupations of Alcatraz and the Bureau of Indian Affairs building in Washington, and as a part of all that, the descendants of those we were digging up let us know very clearly that they didn't like the way we were handling the remains of their ancestors. Today, most of us recognize that we have to balance the efficiency of our data gathering—and indeed, our very gathering of data—with respect for the dead and for the beliefs of their descendants.

This doesn't mean that we don't still have to do fast salvage of burials, but it does mean—particularly since Indian tribes, Native Hawaiians and others, sometimes with archaeological allies, have gotten protective laws passed in many areas—that we have a bit more leverage with those who destroy archaeological sites, and we should, in most cases, be able to negotiate better deals for both the dead and the data they contain. And it means that whatever we do with human remains, and with a tribe's or other group's ancestral sites in general, ought to be worked out in consultation with that tribe or group. As I write this, I'm looking at a November 21, 2004, article from the *Seattle Times* about a big cemetery of the Lower Elwha Klallam Tribe that's being destroyed by bridge construction near Puget Sound. Archaeology is being done, graves are being excavated, the remains removed to a laboratory. Everything is being done in consultation with the tribe, the remains are being stored facing the sunrise in accordance with tradition, and when all is said and done they'll be returned to the tribe for reburial. But there are still major questions about why the project has been allowed to proceed at all; there's a real debate about whether it ought to be abandoned out of respect for the ancestors, and the adequacy of the consultation undertaken by the highway planners with the tribe is being held up for serious scrutiny. Millions of dollars are being spent trying to balance the needs of the project with respect for the dead, and for Klallam culture. Not with respect for archaeological data; the archaeological findings of the excavations being done are interesting and valuable, but archaeology isn't what stirs emotional interest in the site and the conflict. It's the resurgent culture of the Klallam Tribe, and the feeling most people have that the bones of the ancestors ought to be respected. Archaeologists today are responsible for paying close attention to these interests in planning and carrying out their work.

There are still other responsibilities. We're responsible for keeping the people who work with us healthy and safe; this responsibility is enshrined, in the United States, in the laws administered by the Occupational Safety and Health Administration (OSHA). If we dig very deep, our units have to be no smaller than a size specified by OSHA, or we have to shore up the sidewalls. People have to have hardhats if things may fall on them. We need to be careful about dust inhalation and diseases that lurk in the soil, about exposure to heat, about providing sufficient clean water, about reasonable working hours.

We're responsible to landowners. We need their permission to work on their land; we can't let their cows fall into our excavations, we need to clean up after we're done, often backfill our excavations, avoid starting grass fires or breaking down fences.

We're responsible to those who finance and permit our work not only to work efficiently but to carry out the terms of the agreements we sign—contracts, the terms of grants, permits issued by land-managing and regulatory agencies. We need to be able to show that we did what we said we'd do, or that if we didn't, there was a good reason for doing something different.

We're responsible for controlling environmental impacts—not screening our soil into the creek if it chokes the fish or suffocates the plant life, not causing undue erosion, not digging up an endangered species' habitat.

And we're responsible—it's one of our most basic responsibilities—for getting the information we extract from archaeological sites into a form that others can use, which traditionally has meant publishing the results of our work in monographs, books, and professional journal articles. These days there are new ways to share our data—on the internet, on compact disks. Some of us have Web sites and weblogs where we post material. There's vigorous debate in archaeology about what the most effective and appropriate ways are to share data, but the bottom line is this: if we just dig, or otherwise extract data, and put the information away someplace where nobody can use it but us, we haven't done our job.

We also haven't done our job if we haven't seen to the proper disposal of the stuff we excavate—the artifacts, the ecofacts, the human remains, the samples of soil. What constitutes proper disposal depends on a number of circumstances. Often it means permanent retention in a museum, archive, or some other sort of curatorial facility, but some stuff is discarded after analysis, or even destroyed in the process of analysis, and there's quite a range of other possibilities. However we dispose of what we find, though, we need to make sure we do it in an orderly way, and document how it's been done for future reference.

How we dispose of something depends substantially on who owns it. Which is, in a way, another principle.

Ownership

"That belongs in a museum!" the young Indiana Jones mutters near the beginning of *Last Crusade*, about a really neat artifact that the bad guys are trying to make off with. Acting on his belief, Indy makes off with it himself, fleeing the baddies through the rocks, over the desert, over, under, and through a trainload of circus animals. All the watching archaeologists munch their popcorn and nod their heads. "Good boy!"

It's a safe bet that most archaeologists, if they had their druthers, would have all the stuff that comes out of archaeological sites, and all the notes, photos, maps, and digital files created by archaeological projects, safely housed in museums or museum-like facilities. But that's not necessarily what happens, and the fact that it's not what happens isn't solely because there are bad guys who haunt the southwestern deserts or U.S. policy makers who give priority to the Iraqi Oil Ministry over the National Museum.

In the United States, artifacts from private land belong to the landowner, subject to state and local laws. Some state and local laws are pretty restrictive, particularly where human remains are concerned; quite a few states have cemetery and unmarked grave laws that more or less require that graves be left alone, or treated with respect if they must be disturbed. But artifacts, for the most part, belong to whoever owns the land they're found on.

So if you dig a site, or collect stuff off the surface of a site that's privately owned, it's very likely that you'll have to give the stuff back to the landowner, not to a museum—unless, of course, the landowner agrees to donate it. This is the case even if you're digging as part of some CRM project—say, in advance of a federally assisted construction project. The notes, maps, photos, and other records you create in the process of your work are another matter; they're generally understood to be your property, or the property of whoever funds your work, and if there's any federal involvement in your project (as in the example of the federally assisted construction work), there will probably be provision for lodging them in a museum or similar institution.

Artifacts from federal land, on the other hand—land controlled by the Forest Service, the National Park Service, the Bureau of Land Management, any of the military services, the Department of Energy, and so on—belong to the federal government, and the Archaeological Resources Protection Act requires that if they're "of archaeological interest"—which generally means at least 100 years old—they be retained by the government in perpetuity. Requirements for younger stuff are a bit vaguer, but it's still government property, and taking it without permission is theft. There are stringent government requirements for the "curation" of federally owned artifacts and other archaeological material, as well as associated field notes, photos, and the like. Under another federal law, the Native

American Graves Protection and Repatriation Act, ancestral Indian tribal, Native Alaskan, and Native Hawaiian human remains and certain kinds of artifacts defined as "Native American cultural items" must be *repatriated*—that is, given back—to the tribes or groups with whose ancestors they're associated, if such remains or items are found on federal or tribal land, or wind up under the control of an agency or institution that's received federal funds.

So in the United States, exactly who owns the stuff generally depends on who owns the land. It's technically simpler in many other countries that regard all antiquities as the property of the government—part of the governmentally protected "national patrimony" or "national heritage." But practically speaking, it would be pretty intrusive for a national government to claim ownership of everything in the ground that's over, say, 100 years old. As a result, what's actually *regarded* as an antiquity in most countries tends to be rather more narrowly defined than it is in the United States. You're not supposed to pick up a fragment of prehistoric pottery on federal land in the United States without a permit, but if you pick up a chunk of Roman amphora in a vineyard in France, you're unlikely to get into any trouble.

This, incidentally, might be said to be another principle: the more tightly government controls something, the more narrowly that thing is defined, and vice versa. People who favor preserving archaeological sites, historic buildings, and other such cultural resources often call for the U.S. government to beef up its protective laws. If this happened, it's a safe bet that we'd find the government also moving to redefine what's protected by such laws, to cover a much narrower range of sites, buildings, and other things than the law now deals with.

A rather different set of laws applies under the deep oceans. Nations generally control access to archaeological sites (like shipwrecks, and living sites and burial places submerged by rising sea levels and land subsidence) close to their shorelines, and to the wrecks of commissioned naval vessels, but the wrecks of nonnaval vessels in deep water are subject to Admiralty law, under which someone who wants to salvage a wreck may "arrest" it and be awarded exclusive control over it—which is tantamount to ownership.

Who Pays?

Let's talk money. Who pays for people to do archaeology?

Sometimes, the people who do it pay for it, or people pay who support a project out of a personal or other interest. TIGHAR's Amelia Earhart search project, for example, is funded by TIGHAR, a nonprofit organization drawing on the private contributions of interested individuals and occasional sale of media rights. Quite a few institutions and organizations recruit paying volunteers for their projects, and support their work that way. Then there are charitable foundations—big ones like the National Science Foundation and many, many smaller ones, some associated with particular institutions and academic programs—that provide grants for archaeology. Such grants support the bulk of what's referred to as *pure research*— that is, archaeology (or any other form of research) done solely for the purpose of advancing knowledge.

In CRM, most of the money that supports archaeology comes from government agencies and private companies whose plans and projects threaten to destroy or damage archaeological sites—reflecting a principle that's sometimes articulated as "Let the destroyer pay." Under laws like the National Historic Preservation Act and the National Environmental Policy Act, if the federal government has anything to do with a project that may change cultural resources or any other aspect of the environment, the responsible federal agency has to figure out what damage its action really will do, and then take steps to control or make up for such damage. A government agency may fund this work itself, or pass the costs on to the nongovernmental body that's going to benefit from the work. So if the BigPlume Power Company wants to put in a new power plant, and needs to use some federal land or get a federal permit—say, a permit to discharge fill into a waterway, under the Clean Water Act— BigPlume is likely to be required by whatever federal agencies are involved to identify its environmental impacts and do something about them. Identifying impacts will often include hiring archaeologists to do surveys, find sites, and figure out how important they are—for research and other purposes. Then if there's no better way to take care of them—to "avoid, minimize, or mitigate adverse effect" is the commonly used jargon—then BigPlume will probably be required to pay for archaeological excavations, analysis, reporting of results, and long-term care for recovered artifacts, other material, and data. In Admiralty law cases, the salvager of a shipwreck may be required by the Admiralty court to conduct archaeology on the wreck being salvaged, or may elect to do so because it's the responsible thing to do and enhances the value of what's salvaged.

Federal agencies themselves hire archaeologists, as do some state and local agencies and Indian tribes. Many of these archaeologists don't actually do much archaeology in the field—they work in agency environmental offices, or oversee agency compliance with the CRM laws. But they're all involved at least indirectly in doing archaeology, so their salaries and expenses are another source of financial support.

Hundreds of millions of dollars are spent every year in the United States on CRM-based archaeological surveys and excavations, and more or less equivalent amounts are spent in countries like the United Kingdom, other European nations, Australia, Canada, and Japan. Spending on CRM-like archaeology in less wealthy countries is variable, but is generally related to the level of development. International funding agencies like the World Bank, for instance, put money into archaeology both as part of project environmental impact assessment and control, and as a spur to economic development through tourism. In sum, the vast majority of archaeological research today is somehow related to CRM, and its funding is based largely if not entirely on the principle of "Let the destroyer pay."

Archaeology Destroys

Speaking of destruction—archaeology itself is an invasive, destructive operation. We destroy the sites we dig, and they don't grow back—this is why archaeologists sometimes refer to sites as *nonrenewable resources*. Certainly we preserve the information we extract from such sites, and much of the stuff we remove from the ground, but everything else we destroy. This fact becomes painfully clear when a new analytic technique is developed and we realize we didn't keep the information we'd need in order to apply the technique to our data. You can't get a radiocarbon date on your site if you didn't keep anything that's got radioactive carbon isotopes in it, such as burned wood from fireplaces. You can't extract DNA from the food residue on the insides of pots if you've scrubbed all the pots. Analytic techniques evolve with startling rapidity. Today we can learn a tremendous amount from a site that we couldn't even imagine ten or twenty years ago, by studying soil chemistry, for example, and residue in pots and on grinding tools, and by examining pollen and plant remains, and the internal structure and chemistry of bones. It's a safe bet that ten or twenty years from now, archaeologists will have new and—to us—unimaginable technology to apply to understanding a site, if the site's available for them to study. But if we've dug up all the sites . . .

Or it may not be new techniques that are involved, but our choice of those available now. If only we'd used one-eighth-inch screen instead of one-fourth-inch, we'd have found the fishbones we now know were in the site, and gotten a handle on what role fishing played in the economy. If only we'd dug *this* quadrant of the site, taken *that* measurement.

And from a nonresearch standpoint, the damage done by digging may be worse. In the eyes of many an Indian tribe, digging up the ancestors' bones interrupts their journey to the spirit world. While putting them back in the ground with the proper prayers and blessings may allow their journey to continue, their disturbance has nevertheless been an offense that may not ever be entirely mitigated.

In the CRM context, the offense is compounded by the fact that we may be the last archaeologists to have a shot at the site before it's totally destroyed. Often when we fold up our screens and pack up our shovels, the 'dozers are going to roll, and the site's going to be churned up by the road, the levee, the shopping center.

There are several things a responsible archaeologist tries to do in recognition of the destructiveness of the enterprise. First, she tries to dig only sites that are threatened by something. If a site can be preserved in place, it should be. Respect the ancestors that made it and may be buried in it; leave them in peace. Leave the data in the site for some later time, more developed methods, more skilled practitioners.

Second, know what's available. Get on top of the latest new techniques, methods, gadgets, and gizmos when you're planning your work, so you'll know whether you can use them, how to use them, and what to do to collect data in ways that will make it possible to apply all the available analytical approaches. We have a button from the site where we think Amelia Earhart died. It has DNA on it. Earhart's DNA? Maybe, but because we weren't aware when we picked it up that DNA could be extracted from the surface of a button, we failed to put on latex gloves before picking it up and passing it around, so we'll never know; we contaminated it.

Third, try to record all the data you can, even data that aren't relevant to your particular research. Obviously this has to be balanced against doing efficient research; you can't record everything, and you do need to stay focused on your own research objectives. But to the extent you can, try to make a responsible complete record, collect data that others may be able to employ in their research.

Fourth, consult with your peers; ask others what they'd do. Anybody have a hot new technique for recording really fine-grained stratigraphy? For distinguishing between burned roots and fire pits? For analyzing badly oxidized iron artifacts? How would you approach this great big dispersed chert quarry site?

And finally, collaborate; two heads are better than one, particularly if they have different packages of skills, knowledge of different approaches, different (but not too conflicting) interests, knowledge of different kinds of techniques. In the destructive business of archaeology, a team approach is really best.

The last thing to say, though, is don't freeze. Yes, you're going to destroy what you dig. That's the way it goes. Live with it, get over it. Archaeology is like life; if you're going to accomplish anything you have to learn to live with regret, learn from mistakes, and get on with it.

"It," of course, being the archaeology—whatever kind of archaeology you're doing. Let's look next at what that may be, what it's like to do it.

Chapter Four

What's It Like?
The Practice of Archaeological Research

There are several more or less standard things that an archaeologist does in carrying out a piece of research, whether it's "pure" research done to address some important anthropological or historical topic, or research applied to the needs of cultural resource management (CRM).

Administration

Before, during, and after any piece of research, there are administrative tasks that must be done. Getting money, for one thing—usually via a grant or a contract—unless you're independently wealthy or are just doing archaeology for fun. Getting a permit if you're working on land where one is required. Getting necessary background research documents, maps, and equipment. Contacting the owners of the land where you plan to work, to get permission and make arrangements. Maybe hiring and organizing a team.

Nonfield Research

On most projects, the great bulk of research is not conducted in the field; it's done in libraries, archives, on the internet, and in conversations with other people. This is done for its own sake, because you can learn a lot about the past from documentary records and oral history, and for purposes of planning field survey and excavation—figuring out where you're likely to find sites or other things, what they may be like, and how to deal with them. The *Archaeologist's*

Toolkit emphasizes the importance of prefield research by devoting a whole book—Book 1, *Archaeology by Design* by Stephen Black and Kevin Jolly—to the subject. The bottom line is that besides all her other skills, an archaeologist needs to be a good historical researcher—or know her limitations and have access to good help.

In our Earhart research, before we ever sailed to Nikumaroro, the island where we think she wound up, we did extensive research in old newspapers, in archives, and in the published literature. We found, among other things, that Nikumaroro had been colonized between 1938 and 1963, which told us that we should expect to find the remains of the colonial occupation, that we might be able to find living people who had resided there and perhaps knew things of interest to us, and that had there been obvious signs of Earhart's fate lying around, they would have probably been reported. Research also brought us the curious story of Floyd Kilts, published in a San Diego newspaper in 1960, in which he reported having heard about a skeleton being found on the island with a woman's shoe, "American kind."

Often we'll organize the results of our background research into what's sometimes called a *predictive model*. Such a model—which may be constructed at any of a number of geographic scales—simply predicts where we think we're likely to find different kinds of sites based on our research. "Archaic-period sites are likely to be on well-drained soils near springs and streams." "Ritual sites are likely to be on rocky ridgetops with views of the volcano."

Nonfield research doesn't stop when you go into the field. There's a continual interplay between fieldwork and nonfield research. You're constantly learning of new sources of archival or anecdotal information, whose study gives you more places to look in the field, more and different things to look for. In the Earhart case we were finally led to archives on the island of Tarawa and in England that confirmed the story of the skeleton with the shoe, and told us roughly where on the island it had been found; this area naturally became a major target for our fieldwork.

Some CRM archaeologists reduce their prefield research to merely checking lists of sites found during previous studies, like the state historic property inventories maintained by most State Historic Preservation Officers. These are important sources of data— you need to know what previous archaeologists have found—but they're not the only useful sources, and if they're all you check, you may miss a lot of rich, important data. Merely "checking the state inventory" is a sure sign of a lazy archaeologist.

Survey

Field survey serves two purposes. It allows you to find sites you want to study, usually through excavation, and it provides useful research information in itself. If your research is about old agriculture practices in the Western Isles of Scotland, for example, a lot of your fieldwork is going to involve finding and plotting ancient fields

Figure 14. Recording rock art in a cave during survey. *Courtesy www.TexasBeyondHistory.net, Texas Archeological Research Laboratory, University of Texas at Austin.*

and farmsteads, mapping stone walls and crofters' cottages. You may not do much digging at all. Same story if you're trying to figure out the ancient road system that centers on Chaco Canyon in New Mexico. Lots of poring over aerial photos and satellite images, perhaps buzzing about in a light plane or helicopter, lots of walking through the creosote bush and looking for subtle patterns in the contours of the ground.

Survey isn't just a matter of walking around looking for something. It's an organized process involving its own special techniques and skills. You may use specialized equipment, too. If you're surveying underwater, particularly in deep water, you may need to learn how to work with side-scan sonar and sub-bottom profilers. If you're looking for buried sites in alluvial valleys, you may need ground-penetrating radar.

Most survey, though, uses as its prime tool the "Mark-One Eyeball." You just look carefully for evidence of past human activity. This is not as easy as it may seem. My undergraduate mentor, Adan Treganza, used to talk about having to "calibrate your eyeballs" to see things on the ground. I didn't understand what he meant till I moved from northern California, where there was no prehistoric pottery, to southern California where there was. I couldn't see the stuff. People were constantly pointing out potsherds I'd just stepped over (or on) and making me the butt of jokes. And then one day, mysteriously, I could see potsherds as well as anyone; my eyeballs had calibrated.

Although there's value in just taking your eyeballs out for a casual stroll to see what they can see—and all kinds of stories about wonderful things being found that way—most survey is done following some kind of systematic plan designed to make sure that all the ground is inspected at a more or less comparable level of intensity. Usually the members of a survey team will spread out in a line across one edge of the area to be surveyed, spaced at regular intervals—say five or ten meters apart. Then we'll march forward, scanning the ground and any cliffs, stream banks, rock outcrops, and other geographic features we come across. If the ground is obscured by vegetation, we'll dig small holes—*shovel test pits* or STPs—at regular intervals, sometimes screening the dirt we dig out, sometimes just scattering it and looking at it carefully, to see if we find flakes of stone, fragments of pottery, pieces of metal or bottle

Figure 15. A 1x2 meter test unit. Note the stakes and string used to lay out where to dig. The strings are a bit less tight than they ought to be, and I'm showing bad form to be sitting on the sidewall; in a deeper excavation where the wall could cave in, that would be a big no-no. *Photo by Pat Thrasher, TIGHAR.*

glass. We keep careful notes about where we walk and what we see, and when we find something we record it and plot it on a map. We'll usually plot it using global positioning system (GPS) technology, and the more high-tech survey teams keep their notes digitally using personal digital assistants (PDAs) or something similar. We all take more general records, too, maybe keeping a running log or kicking back after work to record general observations. When the survey's done, or before, the team leader pulls everyone's notes together and tries to make sense of them, so as to prepare a report on the whole survey and what's been found. Specific sites are usually recorded on forms designed for the purpose, often following a format developed by a state, provincial, or tribal government agency that maintains a central database of archaeological site data to which everyone working in the area contributes.

We'll give special attention to areas where background research suggests there ought to be something—where the historical maps say the general store used to stand, where our knowledge of prehistoric settlement patterns suggests people would have had a village 2,000 years ago—but we don't ignore the areas where we *don't* expect to find anything. If we looked only where we expected to find things, we'd be creating a self-fulfilling prophesy. It's a safe bet that we won't find things in places we don't look, but that doesn't mean they're not there.

If the survey area is too big or too densely vegetated to inspect completely, we'll do some kind of sample. The most common way to do a sample survey is by walking transects. We'll plot out long linear swaths across the survey area, usually of a standard width—say, 100 meters. We'll walk one of these transects, then skip several and walk another. Sometimes we'll select transects by assigning them numbers and picking from a table of random numbers; other times we'll try deliberately to make sure we're hitting all the survey area's different environmental zones, like hill slopes and stream banks. Then we'll try to extrapolate from our survey data to get an idea of what's probably in the whole area.

Figure 16. Wet-screening excavated soil. *Photo courtesy Rob Edwards, Cabrillo College Archaeological Technology Program.*

While we're doing all this systematic survey, it's a good idea to leave some time for nonsystematic survey, too—just wandering around following hunches. It's sort of discouraging to the scientists in us, but very, very often it's during this sort of random wandering that the most important discoveries are made.

Another important way to find things is by asking people. People whose families or communities have lived in the area for a long time are going to know where old buildings stood, where people did things in the past. They're also likely to have found things representing people who lived in the area in the more distant past—prehistoric artifacts when plowing the south forty, a grave that washed out of a creek bank back in '78. People who collect artifacts for a hobby may have extensive collections from the area that they're willing to show you and let you record, if you treat them with respect. Archaeologists sometimes don't treat such people with respect, though, shunning them as despicable pothunters or unscientific collectors. That's dumb; these people share our interests—they just haven't been fortunate enough to get paid to pursue them. We ought to treat them as colleagues, if we can.

The descendants of those whose sites we're looking for are another group that it's important to talk with. It is, after all, their history we're looking into, their ancestors' stuff we're trying to find. They may or may not have legal ownership rights in what we're looking for, but they almost certainly have emotional investments that ought to be respected. And they may be able to provide very useful information: "Grandma used to say that people would camp along the bank of that creek to collect willow for basket making." Better look closely at the creek bank for signs of habitation and plant processing.

But whatever we do and see, we record it, in words, photos, sketches, and maps. We record what we do, and where we do it. We record the weather, the plants and animals we see, changes in the kinds of soil we see and walk through. We record where we dig shovel test pits, if we do, what shape they are, how wide and deep they are. We record evidence of disturbance to the environment— holes in the ground, recent trash. And of course we record the sites and isolated artifacts we find. *Unless*—and this does sometimes happen—we're asked *not to* by someone whose request we need to respect. Sometimes, for example, we may be accompanied in the

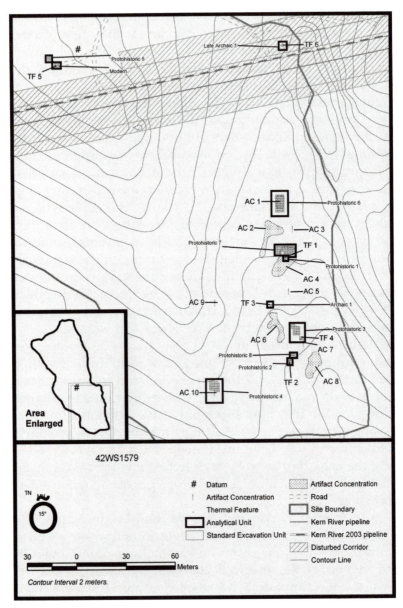

Figure 17. It's all about context. Sites must be mapped before they're excavated, and the excavations are then plotted in. This site is made up of surface artifact scatters, and rather than conduct excavations the archaeologists picked up everything in mapped *analytic units*. At the top, note the right-of-way of the pipeline that's the reason for doing the fieldwork. *Courtesy SWCA Environmental Consultants.*

field by an elder from a local indigenous community, and we may find something that the elder regards as spiritually sensitive, maybe dangerous. He or she may ask us not to take photos, or even not to record the thing at all. We need to try to respect that request, though sometimes it puts us in a bind, since our job, after all, is to make an accurate record of what we encounter. Where there's a conflict between a respected person's desires for confidentiality and our need to record things, we need to talk it through, try to work it out. Sometimes we succeed and sometimes we don't.

What I've just described is a survey on land, in a relatively rural area. Of course things are different if you're surveying underwater, or in a built-up urban area. But even under such circumstances we try to do essentially the same thing—systematically cover the ground, see what we can see, and record it. Of course we can't see the bottom of the ocean 2,500 feet down, but side-scan sonar and robotic submersibles with video cameras can, so we use that kind of technology just as we would our eyeballs, usually dragging or driving them on transects across the seafloor. At shallower depths we may have teams of divers swim transects, sometimes using hand-held metal detectors or other instruments as well as their eyes. In built-up urban areas we may not be able to inspect the ground at all, or may be able to look only at vacant lots and spaces between streets and sidewalks. We may not be able to do much field survey at all; we may have to rely entirely on background research and predictive modeling, at least until the buildings come down and the streets are torn up.

For details about survey, see Book 2 of the *Archaeologist's Toolkit*, creatively titled *Archaeological Survey*, by James Collins and Brian Molyneaux.

Excavation

Excavation is discussed in detail in the *Archaeologist's Toolkit*, Book 3, *Excavation*, by David Carmichael, Robert Lafferty, and Brian Molyneaux. The process is so variable, so specific to the site we're digging, the questions we're asking, and the circumstances under which we're working, that I couldn't possibly do it justice here. But in general, what we try to do in an excavation is to record precisely what's in the ground where we dig, and where it is in both horizontal and vertical space. Because, of course, we're trying to reconstruct what happened on the site, and how what went on there may have changed through time. What exactly we're trying to find out by doing this reconstruction, and hence what we emphasize in doing it, depends on the research questions we're trying to answer. Since excavation churns up the ground we excavate, destroying the information it contains, it's particularly important that we proceed in accordance with a carefully developed plan, usually called a *research design*. The research design spells out the questions we're asking and the hypotheses we're testing, the information we need to address our questions and hypotheses, and the methods we're going to employ to get that information. Survey is guided by research designs, too, but they're especially vital as guides in excavation, because of excavation's destructive nature. See Book 1 of the *Archaeologist's Toolkit, Archaeology by Design*, for details.

The level of precision with which we record things, and the ways we do it, varies widely depending on the type of site we're dealing with, the kind of research we're doing, the questions we're trying to answer, and the circumstances in which we find ourselves. Here are some examples from my own experience.

At the Seven Site on Nikumaroro, there's a hole in the ground where historical evidence suggests a human skull found on the site back in 1940—possibly Earhart's—was buried and later dug up. In 2001 we re-excavated this hole and the pile of coral gravel next to it to see if perhaps some teeth had fallen out of the skull and we could find them. We laid out two excavation units over the hole and pile, and dug them by shovel and trowel in 10-centimeter levels. We passed all the dirt (mostly coral rubble) over a one-quarter-inch screen. We then took everything that fell through this screen and put it through a one-eighth-inch screen. Then we waited till dark and swept all the screenings, and the excavations, with ultraviolet light, in which bones and teeth fluoresce. We recorded everything that turned up—which unfortunately did not include human bones or teeth—as to where it was found in the excavation unit and its depth, and placed it in labeled bags for further study.

At Iras Village in Chuuk, Federated States of Micronesia, Pat Parker and I supervised excavations by the village residents in advance of sewer line construction. We used a huge, mechanized excavator to remove road fill along the side of the village road, down

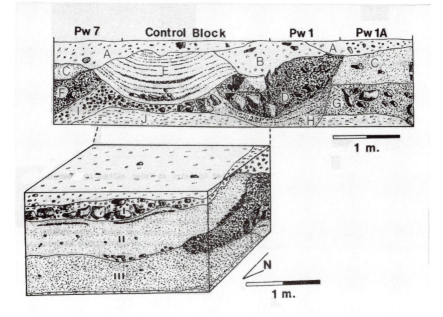

Figure 18. Stratigraphy at Pwpwúnúkkamw. *Drawing by the author.*

to the point at which we began to scrape dark, shell-strewn, sandy *midden*—that is, organic soil representing decomposing organic waste. This was the deposit left from old Iras Village, as it had existed before the Japanese military caused it to be destroyed and covered up by a runway at the beginning of World War II. We then laid out one-by-two-meter excavation units in the trench the excavator had dug, and excavated these by shovel in 10-centimeter levels, running all the sand through one-quarter-inch screen. Everything we found—artifacts, animal bones, plant remains—went into bags labeled by unit number and level, for future sorting and analysis. When we found things like burials and fire pits, we carefully exposed them with trowels and brushes, sketched them and photographed them, then took them apart, bagged them, and continued on. At the nearby Pwpwúnúkkamw Site, we worked in much the same way, except there—where there had been many earth ovens used for cooking breadfruit—we could see natural strata in the soil, so we followed these rather than using arbitrary 10-centimeter levels.

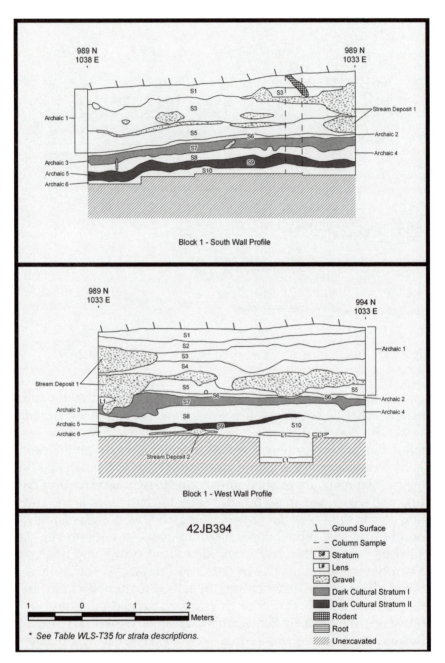

Figure 19. Keeping records is a fundamental part of any fieldwork. Stratigraphic drawings from an excavation unit. *Courtesy SWCA Environmental Consultants.*

At the Buchanan Dam cemeteries on the Chowchilla River in California, which were about to be destroyed by dam construction after several years of controlled archaeological study, I worked in from the edges of each site, and down from the top, with a largish bulldozer until I found the boundaries of each cemetery and had removed most of the overlying midden (as at Iras, the remains of a village, and full of artifacts and ecofacts). Then I formed my team up in a line along one edge and had them scrape the soil down in rough 20-centimeter levels, discarding it without screening, until they hit burials. They dug around the burials, leaving them in place. A two-person transit team was on hand at all times to record the locations of burials as they were found, and each was assigned a number. When enough burials had been found, team members would stop shoveling and clear burials using trowel and brush, with instructions to take, if possible, no more than an hour to expose a burial. Each burial would then be mapped and recorded, disassembled and bagged for future analysis and disposition. Then the shoveling would continue, until the cemeteries had been entirely recorded and removed.

I've never worked at a truly huge site, like the ancient cities of the Near East, Latin America, and Asia, but even in such situations the basic approach is the same; the archaeologist tries to understand the site's organization in horizontal and vertical space, and from this infers how it worked, what people did there, and how it changed through time. At Teotihuacan in central Mexico, for example—which was about the sixth largest city in the world with some 125,000 occupants at its peak some 1500 to 1600 years ago, a great deal of attention has been paid to mapping the site and its structures—pyramids, public buildings, housing compounds, industrial areas, streets, plazas. Mapping alone has taken years, and adjustments continue to be made as parts of the city are studied in greater detail. Excavations of particular structures and groups of structures are planned and carried out with reference to the overall city map, so that gradually a comprehensive picture can be developed of the city and how it changed through time.

Obviously there are vast differences among the techniques represented here, dictated by things like what we were looking for, the nature of the sites, and the circumstances of the dig. At the Seven Site we were looking for teeth, so we had to use very fine-grained techniques. At Pwpwúnúkkamw we had natural strata that we could follow; at Iras we didn't. At Buchanan we were interested in understanding cemetery organization, had already done several years of controlled archaeological research on the sites, and were under the gun, with the sites to be destroyed in a matter of months, so we resorted to drastic and themselves highly destructive measures. At Teotihuacan the importance of spatial relationships among structures and parts of the city has dictated a heavy emphasis on accurate mapping. But in each case the basic approach was the same—not only to recover the stuff we want to study, but to record its original character and location in three-dimensional space.

Analysis

Having collected our data, from survey and/or excavation, and from background research and whatever other studies we've done, we next need to analyze it—figure out what it is we can learn from it, and try to learn it. Even if it's entirely obvious that we're not going to learn anything we're interested in—we dug a site we thought was an ancient religious shrine, and it turned out to be where somebody five or six years ago piled up stones to cover a dead cow—we need to organize our observations in such a way as to share them with our colleagues and with whoever sponsored our work.

Analysis can be as simple as writing up some notes on why we're convinced that what we've found is a five- or six-year-old bovine corpse ("The remains retain a distinct odor . . ."), or it can be a very complex undertaking that involves a wide range of specialists, lots of special technical studies, and often many years of work. The kinds of analysis we do depend on what we have and what we're trying to find out. At a bare minimum it involves cleaning up the stuff we've brought in from the field, assigning numbers to everything, and entering numbers and descriptions in a catalogue for future reference by ourselves and others. It also requires organizing all our field notes into a coherent narrative, explaining what we set out to do, what we actually did, and what we think we learned. We'll need to prepare maps, diagrams, drawings, photographs, and tables to illustrate what we mean. We'll often have to measure, categorize, and describe artifacts, figure out what species are represented by animal bones, mollusk shells, and plant remains, determine the chemistry of soil samples, and find out the ages of samples that can be dated using radiocarbon age determination and other methods.

Figure 20. Lab technician Marty Thomas labels artifacts from the field while Clint Lindsay analyzes data. *Photo courtesy SWCA Environmental Consultants.*

The *Archaeologist's Toolkit* provides good discussions of different kinds of analysis in Book 4, *Artifacts*, by Charles Ewen and Book 5, *Archaeobiology*, by Kristin Sobolik. Very often we'll have to send things out for more detailed analysis by specialists. There are laboratories and experts who specialize in the identification of animal bones, and of butchering marks on them. Others analyze pollen to help reconstruct past environments. Still others are especially expert in "lithics"—that is, stone tools like knives, weapons like flaked stone spearheads, and the waste material left over when such tools and weapons are made. There are experts in shellfish analysis, archaeological soils and geology, metals, glass, ground stone—you name it.

Things turn up in analysis that you never notice in the field. In 2001 we dismantled a pile of *Tridacna* clams—big bivalves—we found at the Seven Site on Nikumaroro and brought the shells home for analysis. When I cleaned them up I was surprised to find that some of them were oddly chipped along their hinge sides. The tip of a little pointed piece of rusted iron we'd found a few meters away fit neatly into some of the chipped openings. Other shellfish were made up of one complete shell, with the matching shell smashed. It looks like someone tried to pry the clams open from the hinge side, and when that didn't work, smashed them open with a rock. Island people are a lot more skillful than that about opening *Tridacna;* most likely whoever collected the Seven Site shellfish was a lot less knowledgeable. Was it Earhart? We don't know, of course, but the shellfish provide an intriguing bit of data that we would never have gotten if we hadn't brought the shells back for analysis.

One kind of analysis the *Toolkit* doesn't discuss much is the analysis of human remains. For that, I can recommend the *Forensic Anthropology Training Manual,*[1] by my sometimes coauthor Karen Burns. Bones can provide a tremendous amount of information if analyzed by an experienced specialist, and subjected to the right kinds of tests. We can learn what kinds of things people ate, how healthy they were, what diseases they had, how long they lived, often how and why they died. We can trace out relationships among people within populations and between populations, and the organization of a burial site often tells us a lot about how the society that produced it was organized. The contents of graves can inform us about social status and occupation. Because they're such rich sources of information, archaeologists are often not very happy about the idea of putting skeletons they excavate back into the ground, or returning them to descendant communities who will probably do so. But most of us have accepted—with varying levels of enthusiasm—the fact that this has to be done, that a decent respect for the presumed wishes of the dead, and the quite certain wishes of living communities that regard themselves as responsible for the dead, demand that human remains, and usually the stuff that was originally buried with them, be reburied. The amount and kinds of analysis that can and should be done on such remains before they go back into the ground are things that we often negotiate about, and the answer depends on things like the importance of the research proposed, the feelings of the community, the letter and interpretation of the law, and the relative political power of the negotiating parties.

Analysis, by the way, is something we need to think about when we're planning our project in the first place. What do we think we're likely to need to analyze, what kinds of special studies may need to be done? What's all that going to cost? These are important factors to consider in preparing a project budget; it's terribly irresponsible to dig stuff up and then not complete its analysis.

Reporting

Reporting what we do and what we learn is a basic archaeological responsibility. We typically describe our surveys and excavations and their results in research monographs, usually with ponderous titles like *Blackenbleue Bayou: An Archaic Alligator Tail-Processing Site in Southwestern Louisiana*. These monographs are usually printed in smallish numbers of hard copies, and increasingly they're produced on compact disks and loaded on web sites. There's a good deal of interest among archaeologists in alternative ways of making basic descriptive data available, and we'll probably see lots of change over the next few decades in the way it's done, but as of 2005, the descriptive paper monograph is still the norm. The idea, of course, is to make the information we've retrieved available to our colleagues, both to show how we've addressed the research questions we set out to address in our work, and to allow others to apply our data to other questions. Reports also demonstrate that we did the work we said we'd do, so they're required by every project

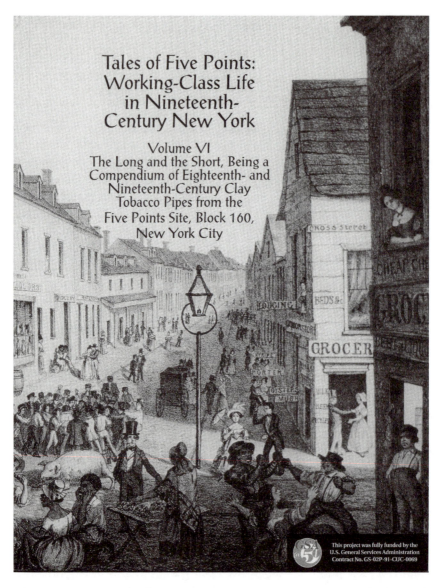

Figure 21. Report of Rebecca Yamin's Five Points Project (one of seven volumes), published by the U.S. General Services Administration. Such reports are sometimes referred to as *gray literature*, because they are not formally published as books or in journals, but they can be massive and sophisticated research documents nonetheless.

sponsor—whether it's a charitable foundation or an agency that hires a CRM firm to dig a threatened site. No report, no payoff.

Assuming we've learned something interesting, either in itself or when considered in the context of other studies, we'll probably publish reports on our work in professional journals, and may write books or contribute chapters to books put together by others. This kind of writing involves less presentation of data and more construction of arguments, drawing on the data we've put in our descriptive volumes. We may also publish popular papers and books—that is, works aimed at the general public, trying to interest people in what we do, explain what we think is interesting, relate it somehow to what we think the public is interested in. And we may put together videotapes and DVDs, television shows, and web sites designed for the same purposes. These are important things to do, if for no other reason than that the public, ultimately, pays archaeologists' wages. More and more of us are writing for the general public—not only popularized versions of our survey and excavation reports, but large-scale summaries of regional history and prehistory, explorations of particular subjects, and even novels. A few examples are given at the end of this book under Further Readings.

Whatever we do or don't do in the way of public-oriented products, though, our basic obligation is to report the results of our work in forms that other researchers, in archaeology and other fields, can use. The *Archaeologist's Toolkit* devotes a full book to the subject of reporting and other forms of presenting results—that's Book 7, *Presenting the Past*, by Larry Zimmerman.

Curation

Curation is a term—made up, I think, in the last thirty years or so—that means taking care of stuff. We've dug all this stuff up from a site, or picked it up from the ground during a survey; curation is what we now do with it.

Curation is discussed in detail in The *Archaeologist's Toolkit*, Book 6, *Curating Archaeological Collections*, by Lynne Sullivan and Terry Childs. The basic idea is that if we're going to collect all this stuff, it doesn't make much sense not to retain it in good shape, so that it can be used for analysis in the future. This goes not only for the stuff per se—the artifacts, the ecofacts, the soil samples—but for the records, too. Our field notes, photographs, maps, computer disks and drives. But archaeology has a pretty poor track record in the curation department; there are many, many horror stories about collections lost, stolen, forgotten and dumped in the trash, or stashed away and found decades later in such horrible shape that they could no longer be used for much.

In a nutshell, we need to make sure that the stuff we've collected—and that we haven't reburied or given back to a community after analysis, or discarded after we've wrung all the useful information out of it (the usual fate of soil samples, for instance)—gets kept by someone who'll keep it safe in perpetuity, that it remains associated with the information that's relevant to it, and that future researchers will have reasonable access to it. Do that, and you've met your curation responsibility as an archaeologist.

Of course, perpetuity is a long, long time, and nobody can really guarantee permanent curation. The excavators of Five Points in New York did a detailed analysis of the stuff they found, produced a six-volume report,[2] and then stored everything in a secure temporary facility while they tried to find an institution to house it over the long term. Unfortunately, the temporary facility was at 7 World Trade Center.

No one, of course—except in this case, Al Qaeda—can be blamed for the kind of thing that happened to the Five Points Collection. An archaeologist's responsibility is to do the best he or she can, in the real world we live in, to make sure that collections of stuff and data are cared for properly. The U.S. National Park Service has published standards for curation[3] that are widely used, and there are a number of other comparable standards used internationally. If your project is likely to produce stuff that will need curation, you need to become familiar with these standards and figure out how you'll make sure they're met. This is another thing that needs to be thought about when you're planning your project. Curation costs money, and it needs to be reflected in your budget.

So, archaeological research typically involves administration, background research, survey and/or excavation, analysis, reporting, and curation. But archaeology as we do it in cultural resource management is a bit different. In fact, in CRM what we wind up doing sometimes isn't archaeology at all, or at least it's more than archaeology. In the next chapter we'll try to get a handle on just what CRM is and how archaeology fits in.

Chapter Five

Archaeology in Cultural Resource Management

We've talked about cultural resource management (CRM) in bits and pieces throughout the preceding chapters. Now it's time to talk about it a bit more cohesively, and to see how archaeology fits into it.

A lot of people think of CRM as a kind of archaeology, archaeology done for money in connection with planning and constructing things like highways and housing developments. Actually, that's the way it's practiced in a lot of places, which is too bad. It *should* be a lot more.

Historic Preservation

At a bare minimum, CRM includes *historic preservation*—which, like CRM itself, means different things to different people. Traditionally, it's meant the management of what's often referred to as the *historic built environment*—old buildings, other structures like bridges and aqueducts, and groups of built things called *districts*. The Old and Historic District in Charleston, South Carolina, is a residential historic district, a group of fine old homes with centuries of associated history. The Vieux Carre (or French Quarter) in New Orleans is a historic district made up primarily of commercial establishments (bars, jazz clubs, restaurants, etc.). Cannery Row on California's Monterey Bay is a historic district associated with the sardine industry, as well as with John Steinbeck's eponymous novel.

Because it's been associated with buildings and other structures, historic preservation has traditionally involved practitioners of architectural history—the study of how architecture has changed through the years in different areas—and historic architecture, which is the practice of architecture using historic buildings. It also, of course, has involved local citizens' groups that want to preserve the built environment that they treasure.

In the United States, historic preservation has been defined more broadly in the National Historic Preservation Act (NHPA). The definition is long and convoluted, but it comes down to the management of any places eligible for inclusion in the National Register of Historic Places. The National Register is a list of significant historic places, which is maintained by the National Park Service.[1] The Register includes a lot more than just elements of the built environment. In the language of the NHPA, it's made up of "districts, sites, buildings, structures, and objects significant in American history, archaeology, architecture, engineering, and culture." In practice, this means that besides the built environment it includes archaeological sites of all kinds, places regarded by Indian tribes as spiritually significant, expansive landscapes, roads and trails, canals, shipwrecks, ships, airplanes, even spacecraft, and it embraces ancient prehistoric places as well as those more recent ones an archaeologist would call historic.

Because historic preservation in the United States is defined to include many kinds of places besides buildings and structures, in this country its practice has come to involve not only architectural historians, historical architects, and local folks who appreciate old buildings, but also historians, landscape historians and architects, local archaeological societies, Indian tribes, other descendant groups, and so on—and, importantly for our purposes, archaeologists. A lot of people use the terms historic preservation and cultural resource management more or less interchangeably. I think this is unfortunate, because it tempts people to forget things that are culturally important but don't happen to be "districts, sites, buildings, structures, and objects" eligible for the National Register. This in turn means that such things are not systematically considered in planning a lot of actions that might affect them.

Collections Management

Collections of cultural objects are one example of such things. The National Museum of the American Indian (NMAI)—the

Smithsonian Institution's spectacular new tribal presence on the National Mall in Washington, D.C.—has a curation facility it calls its "Cultural Resource Center," and rightly so. What's stored and cared for at the Center—baskets, artwork, drums, weapons, tools, clothing, headdresses, ornamentation, religious objects—comprises a resource of tremendous cultural importance to Native American people and to the nation as a whole. But none of the stuff in the Center is eligible for the National Register, because the Register doesn't list museum objects. Reasonably enough, something has to be a "place" to be eligible for the National Register of Historic Places. But collections management—done by a wide range of people with training not only in taking care of collections, but often in archaeology, anthropology, history, materials science, and other fields—is certainly part of cultural resource management by any reasonable definition.[2]

Intangibles

Besides storing and caring for stuff, the NMAI Cultural Resource Center gives tribes a place where they can carry out spiritual activities—prayers, chants, offerings of tobacco and other things to the spirit world. This is important because, as tribes view it, the objects in the Center have spirits of their own, or represent spirits, or are somehow involved with spirits, and those spirits have often been offended by the way the things have been treated. They need to be propitiated, apologized to, made to understand that mistakes have been made but are being redressed.

Such rituals, and the beliefs that underlie them, are examples of what are sometimes called *intangible cultural resources* because they aren't necessarily linked very tightly—if at all—to tangible places and things. In 2003 the United Nations Educational, Scientific, and Cultural Organization (UNESCO) agreed on a *Convention for the Safeguarding of the Intangible Cultural Heritage*[3] which defined this heritage as:

> the practices, representations, expressions, knowledge, skills—as well as the instruments, objects, artifacts and cultural spaces associated therewith—that communities, groups, and in some cases, individuals recognize as part of their cultural heritage.

Figure 22. Some nonarchaeological cultural resources (clockwise from top left): 1. Historic buildings; 2. Historic documents; 3. Culturally valued plants and animals; 4. Culturally valued natural landscapes; 5. Designed historic landscapes; 6. Lifeways and traditions; 7. Culturally distinctive neighborhoods and communities. *Photos by the author or used by permission.*[4]

The definition goes on to list things like oral traditions, language, performing arts, social practices, rituals, craftsmanship, and knowledge about the nature of the universe. Certainly such intangibles are important cultural resources. In fact, it's surely the case that tangible places like sites and buildings are important only because of the way they relate to some kind of intangible value, including the value of knowledge to someone like an archaeologist. Be this as it may, there are certainly important aspects of culture—cultural resources—that exist mostly or entirely in people's heads, and aren't expressed on or in the ground. To the extent such resources are the responsibility of particular professionals, they're the province of cultural anthropologists, sociologists, cultural geographers, and specialists in religion, music, dance, and other expressive arts. But they're mostly the province of the communities in which they play continuing roles.

But What Is It?

So CRM is more than archaeology, and more than historic preservation. What is it?

Back in Chapter One, I defined CRM as:

> a fancy term for trying to take care of what's important to people for cultural reasons—including archaeological sites and artifacts, but also including old buildings, neighborhoods, songs, stories, dance forms, religious beliefs and practices—in the context of the modern world's laws, politics, governments, and economic forces.

We take care of these "resources" in three general ways.

Direct Management of Resources

The folks at the American Indian Museum's Cultural Resource Center are engaged in the direct management of the cultural resources under their care. They make sure they don't rot away (unless they're supposed to), or get stolen, or destroyed by fire or flood. They keep track of them, maintaining lists and catalogues. They regulate who can use them, and what they can be used for. In the same way, a cultural resource manager on a national forest, or in a national park, or on a military base keeps track of and tries to take care of the old buildings, archaeological sites, and other culturally sensitive places on the land he or she (with many other people) is involved in managing. This may involve doing surveys just to find out what's out there, recording it, maintaining records of it, checking it periodically to make sure it's OK. It may involve consulting with other people—the timber folks who want to thin the piney woods, the tank commanders who need to train their people—whose activities on the land may mess up the cultural places. It may mean building a check-dam to stop erosion on the edge of an archaeological site, or replacing the roof on an old building. It's direct management, direct care for resources. It's often called stewardship.

Encouragement

Every year, the Smithsonian Institution puts on the American Folklife Festival on the National Mall in Washington, D.C. Similar festivals are held all over the country, and around the world. They provide opportunities for musicians, artists, craftspeople, and storytellers to perform, to interact, to sell their wares. They encourage communities to keep alive that intangible cultural heritage that UNESCO talks about. This is certainly an important kind of CRM.

Management of more tangible resources can be encouraged, too. *Adaptive use* of historic structures—putting an old structure to a new use while preserving its significant features—is an important part of modern historic preservation and is encouraged in a variety of ways. Some governments provide grants to private owners of historic properties to support their rehabilitation and maintenance. The United States and other countries provide tax incentives for the rehabilitation and reuse of historic buildings and structures, provided approved architectural standards are met. Preservation and conservation easements are purchased from private parties by governments and nongovernmental organizations to preserve significant places from development. The state of Maryland, where I live, has an active program under which private property owners can donate conservation easements to the state and get a tax break for doing so.

Impact Management

Most people, though, when they talk about CRM, talk about management of impacts on cultural resources, and in the United States the focus of discussion is usually on Section 106 of the National Historic Preservation Act. Section 106 doesn't deal with all kinds of cultural resources—its focus is on historic properties. And other nations, and even states of the United States, have impact management systems that work in different ways. But I think Section 106 review is a pretty good example of how impact management tends to work.

Section 106, which has been the law since 1966, requires that Federal agencies—the Corps of Engineers, the Federal Highway Administration, the army, the Federal Communications Commission—"take into account" the effects of their proposed actions on historic properties. Proposed actions—undertakings, in the language of the law—include things that agencies are thinking about doing themselves, things they may help someone else do, and things they permit someone else to do. Here are some examples that I've recently been involved in, directly or indirectly:

- Military training by the Army National Guard on private lands in Louisiana

- Construction of a bridge by the Washington State Department of Transportation, with financial assistance from the Federal Highway Administration

- Construction of a reservoir in Virginia, requiring a permit from the Corps of Engineers to fill in some wetlands

- Construction of towers to hold wireless telephone antennae, requiring the permission of the Federal Communications Commission

In each such case, the federal agency involved has to comply with Section 106, which means going through a review process laid out in regulations issued by the Advisory Council on Historic Preservation. The Council is a tiny little independent federal agency whose main job is to oversee Section 106 review. The regulations are commonly known by the title and section number they're assigned in the Code of Federal Regulations—36 CFR 800.[5] Generally speaking, compliance with the regulations involves the following steps:

1. Getting started. Contacting the State Historic Preservation Officer (SHPO), sometimes one or more Tribal Historic Preservation Officers (THPO), and other parties who may be interested, figuring out how to involve the public in the review, and coordinating with review under other laws like the National Environmental Policy Act. The SHPO is a state official who administers federally assisted historic preservation activities in the state; the THPO is more or less the equivalent in many Indian tribes.

2. Identification of historic properties and effects on them, by figuring out the area or areas where effects on such properties are likely (called the *Area of Potential Effects*, or APE), doing background research, and often doing field surveys and other studies. If places are found that look like they might be eligible for the National Register of Historic Places, they're evaluated using standards issued by the National Park Service. This all results either in figuring out that there aren't any historic properties there, or that there are, and if there are, how they may be affected.

3. If historic properties may be affected adversely by the action, consulting further with the SHPO, THPO, and other interested parties to try to find ways to "resolve" the adverse effects—perhaps by abandoning the action altogether but more often by altering it somehow to reduce damage or by documenting whatever's significant about the property and letting it go. Whatever is decided on is memorialized in a Memorandum of Agreement (commonly known as an MOA), signed by the parties.

4. Carrying out whatever is in the Memorandum of Agreement. In rare cases, though, agreement isn't reached, and the Advisory Council then "renders a comment"—that is,

tells the agency what it thinks the agency should do. The agency doesn't have to do what the Council says—the Council is, after all, advisory—but it must consider the Council's advice at a high level, and explain what it *is* going to do, and why.

Laws

CRM is done because there are laws requiring that it be done. In the United States, the National Historic Preservation Act is one of those laws, and Section 106 is a very important part of that law. But there are others—the Native American Graves Protection and Repatriation Act, the American Indian Religious Freedom Act, the National Environmental Policy Act, and many others. Besides the federal laws there are a number of state, Indian tribal, and local laws that apply under particular circumstances. None of the laws—at least, none of the federal laws—actually requires a comprehensive program of cultural resource management; they deal with the topic piecemeal. Some laws focus on historic preservation, others on religious practice, others on archaeology. It's up to CRM's practitioners to pull it all together.

In other nations CRM—usually called something else using words like "cultural heritage" or "cultural patrimony"—is done under whatever laws apply, for instance, the Ancient Monuments and Archaeological Areas Act in the United Kingdom, the Cultural Properties Protection Act in Japan, *el Ley General de Patrimonio Cultural de la Nación* in Mexico, the Australian Heritage Commission Act down under. There are also international standards for various aspects of CRM established in UNESCO conventions and recommendations like the one on intangible heritage mentioned above. Many nations pay close attention to these standards.

The laws fundamentally structure how CRM is practiced. In the United States, for example, if an archaeological site is found not eligible for the National Register of Historic Places, it's not entitled to any further consideration under Section 106. One may be able to make an argument for doing something with it under another law, but under Section 106, the CRM legal requirement that most federal agencies best understand, the site is a goner. So the processes by which places are determined eligible and ineligible for the National

Register, and the bureaucratic structures, guidelines, and people involved in such determinations, are tremendously important to the practice of CRM.

Where Archaeology Comes In

Archaeologists work in all aspects of CRM, but the vast majority are involved with direct management, impact management, or both.

Major U.S. land management agencies like the Forest Service (which manages national forests), the National Park Service, and the Bureau of Land Management (BLM, which manages vast amounts of public land in the western part of the country) have full-time CRM specialists on staff at several levels—in their Washington offices, in regional offices in places like Denver and Seattle, in national parks and national forests, and in BLM administrative districts and state offices. Most of these specialists are archaeologists. They're responsible for doing whatever they can within the budgets they can get to promote the direct management of resources, and they typically coordinate the agency's Section 106 compliance, or at least advise other agency staff about how to do it. Most other countries have more centralized cultural heritage staffs, in a Ministry of Culture or some equivalent body with government-wide responsibilities.

In the United States, there are also archaeologists on the staff of each State Historic Preservation Officer, and most Tribal Historic Preservation Officers have archaeologists on staff, too. Typically, archaeologists on SHPO and THPO staffs are heavily involved in Section 106 review—looking at agency plans, consulting with them about how to identify and evaluate effects on historic properties, and about how to resolve adverse effects, negotiating Memoranda of Agreement, and monitoring how they're carried out.

And then there are the consulting firms. Some are attached or related to universities and museums, or to nonprofit organizations, but these days most are profit-making private corporations. Sometimes they're independent and focus only on CRM work, like R. Christopher Goodwin and Associates (a big firm) and Nancy Farrell's CRMS (a small one), discussed in Chapter Six. More often they're embedded in larger environmental impact assessment firms—companies that help figure out what the environmental impacts of proposed projects will be, and prepare the documents required by the National Environmental Policy Act. Figuring out the impacts of such projects on the cultural environment—cultural resources—is a natural part of such work. SWCA Environmental Consultants[6] is such a firm; it does all kinds of environmental assessment work, has offices in seventeen western U.S. cities, and does some work in other Pacific Basin countries. Most of its offices have archaeologists on staff—sometimes lots of archaeologists. Other firms, like John Milner and Associates, do both environmental assessment work and project design—in other words, they can assess the environmental impacts of a project and also design the thing. Archaeologists working for such firms are often referred to as *contract archaeologists*, because most if not all the work they do is done under contract with clients—usually agencies or firms that want to undertake some kind of project and need help managing its impacts.

The consulting firms do the bulk of the actual research and other fieldwork in CRM, at least in the United States. Typically a federal or state agency, or a private company that needs to get a federal permit, will put out a *request for proposals* asking for proposals from companies that want to help them, say, assess the environmental impacts of a proposed pipeline. Different companies will offer proposals, and the agency or company will select a winner, sometimes (unfortunately) based just on who submits the lowest bid, sometimes based on which company seems to know best what it's doing and proposes what seems like the most rational approach. A contract will be written up, and the winning company will then do the work.

What's the work? Let me give you an example from my own experience. It's kind of an old example, and a bit exotic because it was done on an island in Micronesia, but it's a good example, I think, because it shows the range of things an archaeologist can wind up doing on a CRM project.

Back in the late 1970s, the islands that the United States had taken from Japan during World War II were administered as the Trust Territory of the Pacific Islands, and the Trust Territory was regarded as a "state" under the National Historic Preservation Act. I was working in the area as a consultant to the Trust Territory government, and my wife, Pat Parker, was living in a village on the island of Wene (then Moen) in Chuuk (then Truk), now part of the Federated States of Micronesia. Pat was doing research in cultural anthropology, as the basis for her PhD dissertation at the University of Pennsylvania.

The Trust Territory government and the U.S. Navy proposed to expand and upgrade Truk International Airport, then a coral runway built over a World War II Japanese bomber base. Which, it turned out, had been built over the old village of Iras, at the base of Mount Tonaachaw, a small, knobby mountain on the northwest corner of Wene. To make a long story short, the government had to do Section 106 review, and I wound up coordinating it. Pat helped, because she was living in "new" Iras Village, in the taro swamp along the inland side of the runway where it had been established at the end of World War II. She knew the people, and spoke the language.

The first steps were to begin consulting with people and doing background research—as a basis for figuring out what, if any, further research might be needed. We talked with government officials and the people of Iras and its neighboring villages, and we looked at literature about the history, archaeology, and traditional culture of Chuuk.

All this told us that Mount Tonaachaw figured importantly in Chuukese tradition—it was where Souwkachaw, the legendary founder of Chuukese society, had built his first meetinghouse, and it was regarded as a spiritually powerful place. There had been villages at its feet since "noomw, noomw, noomw"—long, long ago—and the Japanese military had fortified it. The airport would affect the mountain in many ways, so the whole mountain and its surrounding reefs made up the area of potential effects.

Working with the people of the villages, we then did a field survey. The old village of Iras was invisible under the runway, but old people assured us it was there, so we assumed it was. The nearby village of Mechchitiw was still where it had always been, and a deep midden deposit throughout the village suggested it had been there a long time. There were other ancient sites up on the terraces of the mountain, and one remnant site on the very top, where Souwkachaw had had his meetinghouse. There were also Japanese artillery caves, roads, trenches, foxholes, gun emplacements, even an elaborate latrine. We also documented how the people used the land and reef today—their cultivation and processing of breadfruit, the way they fished, the way they collected shellfish, the way they divided up and shared land—and how these uses would be affected by the project.

As it happened, Tonaachaw had been nominated to the National Register some years earlier, but the nomination form wasn't very complete. Our survey showed that the mountain certainly was eligible for the National Register, both for its association with traditional but ongoing Chuukese culture and for what might be learned from its archaeology. And it showed that the airport project would have serious impacts on what made the mountain culturally and archaeologically significant.

We then mediated negotiation of a Memorandum of Agreement, which provided for some redesign of the airport to protect traditional fishing and shellfishing areas, and financial compensation for the taking of land, breadfruit trees, and fish traps on the reef— much of the compensation in the form of funding a fishing and farming cooperative. It also provided for archaeological salvage, or data recovery, in the old village site and other places that construction would affect.

And then we carried out the data recovery, using heavy equipment to cut down through the old runway and its underlying fill to expose the midden below, testing the midden using hand-excavated 1x2- and 2x2-meter units. And we monitored the mechanized stripping of the whole runway, and hand-excavated burials and features. And excavated sites on the mountain that would be affected, including both ancient Chuukese sites and World War II sites. We described and analyzed the artifacts and ecofacts, the stratigraphy and features and burials, wrote a report, and turned everything we'd excavated over to the villages. Helped them put together an exhibit of some of the material, to go in the Co-op store. And kept after the government to carry out the other requirements of the Memorandum of Agreement.

So what we did on Mount Tonaachaw—and generally what an archaeologist does in CRM—is archaeology, but more than archaeology. CRM archaeologists need to deal with archaeological sites and archaeological research interests, but we have to attend to other kinds of cultural resources too—like, in the Tonaachaw case, traditional fishing, shellfishing, agriculture and land use, as well as World

War II structures and the spiritual significance that the people of the villages ascribed to the mountain. And what we do is structured by the needs of whoever we're working for and with, and by compliance with the law—in the Tonaachaw case the law being Section 106. Archaeologists working in CRM need to understand that, and learn how to work creatively with whatever structure the law provides.

Some contract archaeologists take the position that they really don't need to know much about the laws because it's not their business. Their business, they say, is simply to perform whatever functions their client requires them by contract to perform. This is an understandable position, because if you advise your client too often or too vigorously that he or she is wrong about what the law requires, you're likely not to get another contract. But it's not uncommon for a client to *be* wrong—to not understand what the law really requires—and I don't think you're doing your client a service in such a case to just say "Yessir" and march off to do it. You ought to know the CRM business better than your client, and give the client the best possible advice.

Clients, contractors, the CRM business. If these kinds of roles and functions still seem a little weird, maybe it will clarify things to look at what archaeologists actually *do* in CRM.

Chapter Six

Who Does What? Archaeological Roles in Cultural Resource Management and Beyond

Most archaeologists would probably be happiest doing research all the time, but few if any of us do that. And when we are doing research, we typically assume more or less specialized roles; almost nobody, as an individual, carries out the whole research enterprise. When you're thinking about doing archaeology, it's useful to think about the different roles that archaeologists fill, or that relate somehow to doing archaeology. Some of them will probably be more comfortable fits for you than others. In this chapter we'll outline some of the major roles that people play in and around archaeology, with an emphasis on those related to Cultural Resource Management.

The Academic Archaeologist

The classic place for an archaeologist to be employed is somewhere in academia, usually as a university professor. Even Indiana Jones is portrayed as a professor, with lots of adoring young students of the opposite sex. Nice work if you can get it.

Many archaeologists are employed in academia—not only in universities but in public and private colleges, community colleges, even secondary schools. There are a few archaeologists who've qualified as primary school teachers and find ways to wrap archaeology into the curriculum. But universities and colleges are where most academic archaeologists work.

An academic archaeologist, of course, doesn't do archaeological research all the time. He or she must naturally teach, though as a rule the higher up you are in the academic system, the less teaching you do and the more you're allowed, and expected, to do research. A community college teacher may be able to do research in the form of a *field school*—teaching students to do archaeology by doing it—but most of his time is spent teaching basic anthropology, or maybe sociology or history. A university professor, on the other hand, especially a professor who's been in the system long enough to get tenure, is likely to teach only a few classes, and those will be mostly graduate seminars. She'll not only get time to do research, and the opportunity to seek research grants through the university's grant-getting machinery, she'll be *expected* to do it, and to publish the results. In fact, she will have had to do a good deal of research, and published some reasonably well-received papers, to get tenure in the first place.

Besides research and teaching—which of course also involves preparing classes, grading exams and papers, and counseling students—the academic archaeologist has a range of administrative chores. She'll sit on committees making decisions about hiring and firing, class assignments, allocation of lab space and offices, funding research and scholarships, and a host of other things that her department—in the United States, usually a department of anthropology—needs to do to keep operating. And there are inevitably political matters to contend with—if not big politics like organizing rallies in support of important causes, then campus politics like competing for the best lab space or the most student assistants.

The Museum Archaeologist

The other place people usually imagine archaeologists being employed is in museums, and some archaeologists are indeed employed there. A museum archaeologist is naturally going to be involved in managing a museum's collections, sometimes in developing exhibits, often in giving lectures and classes at the museum or at academic institutions with which the museum is affiliated (museums are often parts of major universities). He may specialize, for example, primarily in registration (keeping track of the museum's collections) or in curation (managing the collections themselves). Museums also employ conservators—technical specialists who know how to keep particular materials like leather or feathers, iron or wood in good condition, and restore damaged material. Many museum archaeologists are primarily educators, designing exhibits and teaching material to help visitors learn about the past, leading tours, giving seminars. Like an academic archaeologist, though, the higher up the professional pecking order the museum archaeologist gets, and the more prestigious his museum is, the less he's likely to be involved in such nitty-gritty work, and the more he's going to be able to do research—until he moves into museum administration, at which point he probably won't have time to do research at all.

The CRM Researcher

But most archaeologists don't work in academia or museums. These days, most people who identify themselves as archaeologists work somehow or other in CRM. Many of these do quite a lot of research; in fact, that's mostly what they do. The research is *applied research*, however. That is, any given survey or excavation probably isn't one that the archaeologist has chosen to do because of her own research interests; it's one that a client needs done. Rebecca Yamin, who ran the Five Points excavation for John Milner and Associates, wasn't dying to study a nineteenth-century slum in New York—though that's what she and her colleagues did. They did it because the General Services Administration needed to build a new courthouse that would wipe out the Five Points site. Matt Seddon and his colleagues at SWCA did a comprehensive archaeological study of a swath of land running clear across Utah and down into California, but not because they wanted to compare and contrast how ancient communities related to the various kinds of environment along the transect through time—though that's what they did. They did it because the Kern River Pipeline Company wanted to put in a pipeline and needed the permission of the Bureau of Land Management to do it.

Most archaeologists who work as CRM researchers are employed by private consulting firms. SWCA, for example, employs about 120 archaeologists in seventeen offices across the western United States. They typically do two kinds of work—surveys (often including limited test excavations) to determine what damage a given project will do to archaeological sites, and excavations or other studies designed to mitigate—that is, reduce or make up for—that damage. Sometimes they do general survey of a large land area—a military training area, for example, or a national forest—to help whoever manages the area figure out what archaeological sites it has to manage. If things go as they should under the CRM laws (see Chapter Five), the archaeologist should be working with other specialists—cultural anthropologists, perhaps, and historians or architectural historians, biologists and geologists, and water resource experts—in a program of interdisciplinary research. She'll also have to relate the archaeology she's doing to the client's needs, to relevant laws and regulations, and to the interests of other folks like descendant communities and the general public. The CRM researcher's life isn't nearly as cloistered as that of her academic contemporary, and although she'll certainly publish monographs and research articles, a lot of her research results will be reported in things like environmental impact statements rather than academic journals.

Rebecca Yamin provides an example of how a CRM researcher's career may develop. Becky studied anthropology as an undergraduate at the University of Pennsylvania in the early 1960s, and found archaeology particularly interesting. When she graduated she hoped to get into Peruvian prehistory, but as things worked out opted to study modern dance in New York. But she also started work on a Masters Degree at New York University (NYU), and there studied under Bert Salwen, one of the founders of CRM archaeology in the United States.

Becky got married, and had her first child at about the time she got her Master of Arts (MA) degree. Not thinking of herself as scholarly, she didn't plan to go on for a PhD, but taught introductory classes at Rutgers University. She found that she loved teaching—communication has turned out to be one of the major themes of her professional life.

At that time the Rutgers Archaeological Survey Office (RASO) did contract archaeological fieldwork for various clients. Becky associated with RASO in the early 1970s, and soon was working on the Raritan Landing project, a large data recovery program at a New Jersey historic site. She was originally hired primarily to write overdue reports, and found that she enjoyed it—not entirely surprising to her, since she'd long been an avid fiction reader.

Becky became increasingly involved in contract work, mostly at historic sites, mostly involving stratigraphic analysis and writing—while having another baby, teaching at several colleges, getting a divorce, and in 1976 enrolling in the PhD program at NYU. She supported her dissertation research by working as an archivist/historian for a civil engineering company in New York City, her introduction to corporate culture and to writing for a lay audience.

Through the 1980s Becky supported herself and her two children doing part-time teaching, part-time writing, and increasingly full-time CRM archaeology, serving as *coprincipal investigator*—that is, sharing supervisory responsibility—on survey and excavation projects on Staten Island. In 1988 she completed her PhD with a dissertation based on Raritan Landing, and at the same time took charge of developing an educational and interpretive element for data recovery at Morven Museum and Gardens in Princeton, New Jersey.[1] On this project, she says, she began to develop her voice as an interpreter of the past.

Recruited in 1992 by John Milner Associates (JMA), a historic preservation firm,[2] Becky has continued to direct increasingly complex projects in the mid-Atlantic states, notably the analysis and interpretation of Five Points. She has developed a distinctive writing style that features what she calls *narrative vignettes*. Rather than simply describing a body of archaeological data, she literally writes a story about it. She finds that this is a good way to communicate both with the public and to nonarchaeological specialists. She says:

> For me the creation of the vignettes is a method for figuring out what you know as well as what you don't know. Their purpose is not as much to make archaeological results more palatable (although they do that) as it is to understand what we have learned from the archaeology and the history together. While it is, of course, gratifying to know that we are reaching lay audiences with these various narrative approaches I am proudest of finally reaching some historians, who have paid quite a lot of attention (both negative and positive) to our findings at Five Points. Writing—and constructing the past—more like they do seems to make all the difference.[3]

Today, Becky is employed as a Senior Project Manager in JMA's Philadelphia office. She has scores of publications to her credit, and is working on popular books about Raritan Landing and the archaeology of Philadelphia.

Of course, not every CRM researcher's career is as eventful or accomplished as Becky Yamin's, but it's not unusual to find people like her—smart, talented, hard-working—who have developed stable, reasonably well-paying jobs doing productive research in the context of CRM. Like Becky, most rather fell into what they're doing while preparing to do something else—usually academic archaeology—and found that it really wasn't a bad way to make both a living and a contribution to society. Like Becky, most do much of their work in a particular area, on whose archaeology they often become leading experts. And like Becky, as they become more senior, they often share their expertise widely with both the academic community and the public.

The Archaeological Businessperson

A successful CRM researcher is likely to evolve into an archaeological businessperson, perhaps climbing the corporate ladder in an environmental planning firm like JMA or SWCA, or perhaps by forming his own company. In such a role, the archaeologist becomes deeply involved in a lot of things besides archaeology—contract negotiations, employee relations, real estate transactions, equipment purchases, cost-containment policies, accounting, taxes.

Chris Goodwin is a successful archaeological businessperson. At Tulane University in the late 1960s, Chris double-majored in political science and anthropology. He graduated in 1971 and headed for the Caribbean, where he fell into doing archaeological fieldwork with Interamerican University. Realizing that "I needed graduate study to continue my lifestyle," Chris enrolled at Florida State University and got his Master's degree there in 1974. He was awarded his PhD by Arizona State University in 1979.

But as usual in CRM, the procession of degrees doesn't tell us much about how Chris came to be doing what he's doing today—serving as president and chief executive officer of R. Christopher Goodwin and Associates, Inc.[4]

Directing a salvage project in Puerto Rico that was voluntarily funded by the developer whose project would destroy the site, Chris first had to begin wrestling with the problems of balancing preservation and development that are so basic to CRM. At Florida State he was in one of the most active applied archaeology programs in the country at the time, many of whose graduates went to work for federal agencies. But Chris was intent on an academic career.

Chris found work at the Smithsonian Institution with the renowned archaeologists Clifford Evans and Betty Meggers. He did research in Latin America, but then found himself working as a museum archaeologist—a job he didn't like nearly as much as fieldwork. He began applying for the only other kind of job that occurred to him—in academia.

But the academic job market wasn't very good in the late '70s. The jobs Chris was offered involved huge teaching loads, little support for research, and a pauper's pay. And at the same time, federal agencies (at least as Chris recalls it) were beginning to get serious about complying with Section 106. Chris says:

> I had an epiphany—I could do more field work and have more fun, travel, and just maybe make a better living in the private sector. I moved to New Orleans, to the heart of the oil patch to establish my practice, and began working for oil and gas companies. After a few years of struggling, things took off, and I've never looked back.[5]

"Things took off" means that he got more and more contracts to do surveys, data recovery, and other kinds of CRM work, from more and more agencies and private firms, over a wider and wider area. So his operation rapidly got bigger and more complicated; he hired more and more people with more and more wide-ranging specializations—not only archaeologists but architectural historians, historians, archivists, folklorists, landscape architects. He opened branch offices, and eventually moved his headquarters to Frederick, Maryland, where he converted an old house into his office building. When his operations got too big for that, he rehabilitated an old (and historic) glass factory to share with other entrepreneurs. Today, Goodwin and Associates is a multimillion-dollar business with offices in Frederick, New Orleans, and Tallahassee, working in terrestrial and underwater archaeology, architectural history, historical architecture, planning, and a wide range of other CRM fields. The firm has been given awards by everyone from Ann

Arundel County, Maryland, to the U.S. Small Business Administration and the National Trust for Historic Preservation. Arizona State University recently named Chris one of its thirty or so "distinguished alumni."

What has equipped Chris to run a business like this? He says he likes solving real-world problems, teaching businesspeople to appreciate preservation. He enjoys the wide range of work involved in his business; he's worked on Babe Ruth's boyhood home, shipwrecks, early plantation sites, and prehistoric sites all over the country and in the Caribbean. And he enjoys the creative political aspects of the work—setting precedents and influencing government policy.

Having spent some time observing Chris in action, I can also say that he's a helluva businessman; he speaks the language of businesspeople, and they speak his. But he's still very much an archaeologist. Hanging around his office, I've been impressed at how deeply he gets involved in technical discussions with the archaeologists who run the company's various field projects. Though most of his work time is spent on the business end of the business—getting out the proposals, negotiating the contracts, making sure they're properly administered, that the money's properly accounted for, that payrolls are met and taxes paid, that the heat stays on in the buildings—he's intellectually engaged by the archaeology his people do, and after over twenty years in business, he's still excited about it.

Most CRM companies aren't as big as Goodwin and Associates. CRMS,[6] for example—the acronym stands for Cultural Resource Management Services—does a few hundred thousand dollars' worth of business most years, operating out of a compact office in Paso Robles, California. Nancy Farrell is the president of CRMS, and works mostly in California and the Pacific Islands.

As an undergraduate at UCLA in 1966, Nancy got started in salvage archaeology at a big historic Chumash Indian cemetery that was being wiped out by residential construction. In those days, UCLA had an Archaeological Survey that did contract and volunteer surveys and salvage work as well as supporting student research. Nancy worked with the Survey through the early '70s, taking part in and supervising field and laboratory projects all over Southern California. As the federal and state environmental and

CRM laws began to be put into effect, jobs—large and small, short-term and long-term—began to open up in government agencies and private firms, and Nancy began making a living in such jobs while doing graduate studies at UCLA.

After a short stint with the Bureau of Land Management in the California Desert, Nancy went to work for a large planning firm working mostly on power plant design and environmental impact assessment. She also began to get involved in field projects undertaken by colleagues in the islands of Micronesia—on Guam, in the Northern Mariana Islands, on Ulithi Atoll—and doing intensive archival research in connection with these studies. She found a lot to interest her both in island archaeology and in documents research.

In 1979, Nancy was working as an archaeologist for the California Department of Transportation when the U.S. Air Force and Army Corps of Engineers began planning to deploy MX missiles—multi-warhead ICBMs—at Vandenberg Air Force Base on the California coast. They needed someone to coordinate their compliance with Section 106 and other CRM review laws. Nancy got the job and worked at Vandenberg for three years, preparing scopes of work for surveys and excavations, supervising contractors, reviewing reports, and consulting with Indian tribes and others who were concerned about what missile deployment could do to cultural resources. When the MX job wound down in 1982, she moved to the Corps' Los Angeles District office and helped coordinate Corps CRM work throughout Southern California and much of the U.S. Southwest. This involved both Corps construction projects and projects done by others with Corps permits—a growing and very complicated business.

Nancy remained with the Los Angeles District until the late 1980s, and then spent a year for the Corps on Kwajalein Atoll in the Marshall Islands, doing surveys and data recovery in advance of construction associated with missile testing. Here she worked not only on traditional Marshallese sites, but on sites from World War II—something that would become one of her areas of specialization.

In 1989, in one of those reorganizations that government archaeologists learn to live with, the Corps dispensed with some of its archaeologists, including Nancy. After a bit of uncertainty, she and a colleague took the plunge into the private sector and formed

CRMS. Many of their early jobs were pretty ordinary—surveying a pipeline right-of-way here, a road widening there. But Nancy's experience in archival work, Pacific Island archaeology, and the archaeology of World War II gave her an advantage in proposing to work on some unusual projects, like a study of World War II sites on Tinian Island in the Mariana Islands, from which the bombers *Enola Gay* and *Bock's Car* took off to drop atomic bombs on Hiroshima and Nagasaki. She came to specialize in work for the Defense Environmental Restoration Project at Formerly Used Defense Sites—with the sonorous acronym DERP/FUDS—where she does archival, oral historical, and archaeological studies of historic places that may be affected by cleaning up environmental waste and hazards.

Today, Nancy has developed a special niche dealing with World War II archaeology, history, and oral history, becoming a very good interviewer who seems to be able to develop real bonds with veterans. Her contract work has been profitable enough to free up some time to volunteer on projects that lack financial support—for example, helping the government of the Solomon Islands develop plans for historical tourism at Guadalcanal's World War II sites.

Chris Goodwin and Nancy Farrell run very different kinds of operations, on very different scales, but there are things they share that are common to all CRM businesspeople. They respond to requests for proposals issued by government agencies and other potential clients; they prepare proposals to carry out work, and compete with other firms to get contracts. They negotiate contract terms, and then oversee the conduct of the work each contract calls for. They maintain infrastructures of personnel, equipment, supplies, and facilities to support their work, and concern themselves with budgets, taxes, and human resource matters. They continue to be involved in fieldwork—Nancy a good deal more directly than Chris—but much if not most of the average workday is spent in managing their businesses. Neither controls the location or nature of his or her work; they have to be responsive to client needs. But each has nevertheless been able to focus on areas of special interest—Southeastern U.S. and Caribbean prehistoric and historic archaeology in Chris' case, World War II archaeology and oral history in Nancy's. And each has built a reasonably stable and satisfying career, employed a lot of archaeologists and others, and made significant contributions to both archaeology and other aspects of CRM.

The Archaeological Bureaucrat

CRM is done largely because of laws enacted by governments, so government agencies do a lot of CRM and oversee far more. As a result, quite a few archaeologists are employed as government agency officials—that is, as bureaucrats. In the United States, land management agencies like the Forest Service and Bureau of Land Management, the military services, and the big construction agencies like the Army Corps of Engineers have dozens of archaeologists on their staffs. Every State Historic Preservation Officer (SHPO) has at least one archaeologist, and usually several. Large state construction agencies like departments of transportation also hire lots of archaeologists. In other countries, CRM archaeologists tend to be less widely distributed across the government agencies; most countries concentrate them in ministries of culture or their equivalents.

Most U.S. agency archaeologists start their government careers in state, regional, or district (local) offices, usually in an "environmental shop" that's primarily involved in environmental impact assessment work. Often they're recruited out of the ranks of CRM researchers and shovelbums (see below). They may initially do quite a bit of fieldwork, maybe looking in on contractors the agency's hired to do projects, or who've been hired by private companies the agency's considering letting do something with the land it administers (like drill for oil, or put in a pipeline). Or they may do surveys of small projects the agency's considering, or incrementally survey the lands the agency administers. They may work with law enforcement people on stopping pothunting and vandalism—helping document the damage done, figuring out who's doing it, and bringing them to justice or trying to persuade them to change their ways. They may be assigned (or volunteer) to represent the agency in working with Indian tribes or other groups with traditional rights to or interests in the land the agency manages.

Gradually, the agency archaeologist will find himself doing more and more CRM work that's not strictly archaeological—dealing with other kinds of cultural resources and interpreting laws and regulations (see Chapter Five). This kind of broadening of perspective is pretty much a prerequisite to professional advancement in the world of CRM bureaucracy. Advancement occurs in one of two directions; either one moves from the local to the regional level and perhaps ultimately to the agency's Washington, D.C., office as its Federal Preservation Officer—coordinating the agency's whole CRM program, or one broadens one's perspective into other areas and becomes a more general manager—a district manager in the Bureau of Land Management, a district ranger in the Forest Service, a national park superintendent. In SHPO offices there tend to be fewer opportunities for advancement, as a result of which there tends to be pretty rapid turnover. In fact, there's pretty rapid turnover throughout the government sector; people move from job to job a lot.

As an undergraduate at California State University Long Beach in the early 1970s, Claudia Nissley was fascinated by archaeology, and imagined compiling data from the many salvage excavations then underway and applying them to answering important questions about human culture. Unable to pursue these ideas very far, Claudia volunteered on field projects, and around the time she got her BA in 1972, she got a paying job, too—with one of the earliest of the for-profit archaeological contracting firms. But contracts were thin, and one day the firm informed its employees that it could no longer pay them. Still a starry-eyed idealist, Claudia with a few others continued to work without pay on threatened sites. It was a hand-to-mouth existence, to say the least.

Eventually deciding that there was no future in this kind of thing, Claudia sought a graduate degree at the University of Colorado. She was surprised to find that her work in what was then just beginning to be called cultural resource management didn't gain her any respect. The prevailing wisdom among academics was that no "real" archaeologist would get involved in such work, and that the data it produced were worthless. Some archaeologists retain this attitude today.

Claudia finished her MA in 1976, by which time she had a job at the Museum of Northern Arizona, doing surveys for research and planning purposes in Arizona, New Mexico, and Utah. But in 1979 she thumbed her nose at academia and jumped into full-time CRM as Forest Archaeologist on the Willamette National Forest in Oregon—where a lot of logging was going on. She supervised ten archaeologists and about 35 technicians doing fast surveys of areas where timber cuts and haul roads were planned, finding sites and trying to route the ground disturbance around them. She found time for studies, however, entering the PhD program at the University of Oregon.

Like many CRM professionals in government, Claudia found that her job was very dependent on how the political winds were blowing. Ronald Reagan's presidency was a very good time for loggers, but not so for obstructionists like archaeologists. Labeled as such by her forest supervisor, Claudia saw the handwriting on the wall and skipped back to Colorado in 1982, landing a job with the State Historic Preservation Officer (SHPO)—the Colorado Historical Society.[7]

Claudia spent four years coordinating the state's avocational archaeological program—working with amateur archaeologists all over the state. Then she got another federal job, this one supervising the western office of the Advisory Council on Historic Preservation[8]—the tiny federal agency that oversees Section 106 review.

At the Council, Claudia's staff comprised a couple of archaeologists, an architect/attorney, a historian, and a secretary. They were trying to make sure that every agency of the U.S. government operating west of the Mississippi River and throughout the Pacific "took into account" the effects of their actions on historic properties, as Section 106 requires. An exciting, challenging job that expanded Claudia's horizons beyond archaeology, but like every federal job, a creature of politics. Claudia lasted twelve years at the Council before running afoul of the agency's leadership and resigning in 1998.

Once you've worked in a senior position at the Advisory Council, there aren't many places to go in American CRM that don't seem like steps backward. Like others in her position (me, for instance, ten years earlier), Claudia went into private practice, consulting and teaching about Section 106 and other aspects of CRM. Such work is a feast or famine proposition, and Claudia experienced both until 2004, when she got another government job—this time as SHPO for the State of Wyoming.[9]

Which is where you'll find Claudia as of early 2005 as I'm finishing this book. She manages an operation with close to a million-dollar annual budget and some fifty full-time and part-time employees—archaeologists, architectural historians, historians, and support staff. Supervising Wyoming's state archaeology program is only one of her duties; she also oversees the state's participation in Section 106 review, a Records Office that maintains a statewide historic property database, nominations to the National Register of Historic Places, and the administration of grants and tax credits for the rehabilitation of historic buildings. She also has a team of field researchers that help the State Department of Transportation and other state agencies that have CRM-related responsibilities. In her free time, what there is of it, she's working on a graduate degree in environmental law, and raises horses and sled dogs.

Russ Kaldenberg is another archaeologist who's built his career in government. Russ did graduate work at California's San Diego State University in the 1970s, and worked with an archaeological contracting operation, gaining a working knowledge of CRM law and practice. He got his Master's degree in 1974, and in 1976 he was hired by the Bureau of Land Management (BLM).[10] BLM manages vast tracts of federal land, and had come to realize that to comply with the new environmental and historic preservation laws it needed expert staff. Quite a few archaeologists got jobs in BLM in the mid- to late '70s.

Russ was hired as a Resource Area Archaeologist, riding herd on hundreds of thousands of acres of the California Desert, largely unexplored by archaeologists. Sites in the desert—Russ knew there were lots of sites, he just didn't know what or where they were— were subject to ongoing destruction by artifact collectors, off-road vehicle traffic, and plain vandalism, as well as by all kinds of construction projects. Russ's job was to find sites, record them, and figure out ways to protect them. He also contracted for surveys and data recovery projects, and supervised the firms and institutions that got the contracts.

In 1978 BLM reorganized, and Russ became California Desert District Archaeologist. He supervised archaeologists in different administrative areas of the desert—some 12 million acres—as they developed the cultural resources part of a plan for the area's management. In 1983, another reorganization sent him first to another job in BLM and then out of the agency altogether. This is not unusual; U.S. government agencies reorganize often, which can make it hard for an archaeological bureaucrat to maintain continuity.

Russ spent two years as Regional Archaeologist with the Forest Service[11]—an agency of the U.S. Department of Agriculture—in Wisconsin. Then he got another BLM job in California, this time as head of an interdisciplinary team working on ways to manage roadless wilderness areas. Having thus gained his spurs as a general resource manager, two years later he took over a whole resource area. He stayed in this job from 1988 until 1993, when the job of BLM State Archaeologist became open and Russ got it.

Russ's actual title was State Archaeologist/California Indian Coordinator/Paleontologist—he was responsible for overseeing BLM's CRM programs throughout California, coordinating with Indian tribes on all matters of mutual concern, and dealing with fossils. He was based in the state capital, Sacramento, while his long-suffering wife, Judyth Reed was by now a BLM Resource Area Archaeologist in Ridgecrest, across the Sierra Nevada. They maintained a commuter marriage for the next ten years. Russ was responsible for a tremendous range of things—budget allocation, budget planning, staffing, consulting with the State Historic Preservation Officer and other agencies, administering permits for research and consulting services, compliance with Section 106 on drilling for oil, gas, and geothermal energy, and issuing rights of way for pipelines and power lines. Russ also promoted surveys to identify archaeological sites that *weren't* obviously threatened, to get a handle on what BLM had to manage in the state, and he became a strong advocate for organized cooperation with Indian tribes. He also found time to be appointed by the governor to the California Historic Resources Commission and to serve in various offices, including the presidency, of the Society for California Archaeology.

In 2003, Russ finally left BLM and joined Judyth in Ridgecrest, becoming Command Archaeologist and Native American Coordinator for China Lake Naval Air Weapons Station—a high-security base with a vast assortment of archaeological sites, tribal spiritual places, and historic structures.[12] Russ is looking toward retirement in the not-too-distant future, but is heavily involved in working with elders in nearby tribes, helping them visit places they lived in and used as young people, from which they've been excluded for decades, and recording their stories. He also serves on the board of directors of a local museum and a cultural association, and recently created a curatorial facility for China Lake collections, staffed by volunteers from the base and the surrounding community.

The life of a CRM bureaucrat can be frustrating. You can spend an awful lot of time in a cubicle shuffling papers, reading other people's reports. And—particularly in the United States—you're typically part of a large organization whose priorities are based on lots of things other than the interests of CRM. This can mean that you can spend a lot of time building a program, only to have it all evaporate because of some new direction from Congress or the White House, or a new regional director who decides to reorganize. On the other hand, you can have a lot of influence over how archaeological sites and other cultural resources are managed in your region or agency. That can be exciting and satisfying, and make a real contribution to archaeology and more broadly to society.

But this kind of influence can also tempt you to become a petty despot, insisting that contractors working for your agency or the companies that seek permits from it, or everyone working in a state if you're employed by the SHPO, do things your way or risk lost permits, long delays in review of reports, and other expensive and time-consuming complications. It's also possible to fall into rote patterns of thinking and doing things. You have all these projects, all these pieces of paper, flowing over your desk, and you begin to find routine ways of dealing with them. These routine procedures may become set in your mind and your organization, until you and everyone around you come to believe they're the only ways of doing business. Avoiding these tendencies can be a psychological challenge.

The Shovelbum

Quite a lot of people these days work as *shovelbums*, that is, as archaeologists who don't evolve—or at least don't do so very quickly—into businesspeople or bureaucrats, but just keep doing archaeology on CRM projects. They often travel from project to project—hence the name. Some have business cards that read "Have Trowel, Will Travel." Some have advanced academic degrees, but many don't. A lot of people shovelbum for awhile when they're fresh out of college with an undergraduate degree; bum around awhile deciding what to do next with their lives, and some decide to just keep doing it.

When they feel like being formal, shovelbums go by the title Archaeological Field Technician (AFT), and there's an AFT job de-scription published by the U.S. Department of Labor:

> Provides technical support to professional archaeologist, uti-lizing a basic understanding of anthropological and archaeo-logical field techniques in connection with locating, testing and evaluating cultural resource sites. Conducts prefield office re-search, field surveys and site testing, using a variety of refer-ence materials, interviews with source individuals, aerial photographs and technical instruments. Searches areas of pro-posed projects for evidence of historic and prehistoric remains. Determines exact location of sites and marks them on maps and aerial photographs. Records information on site survey form and prepares an archaeological reconnaissance report needed for evaluation and management of the project. Insures that work assignments are carried out in safe and timely man-ner according to established standards and procedures. Reviews work in progress and reports to superiors relative to the comple-tion date and other standards set in report. Cleans and catalogs artifacts recovered from inventories and excavations.[13]

There are Web sites[14] that cater to shovelbums—notably www.shovelbums.org, which lists jobs, field-training opportunities, and the like. There are colleges that specialize in technician train-ing, notably Cabrillo College in California.[15] There are cartoon books about the shovelbum's life.[16] There's even a union—the United Archaeological Field Technicians (UAFT)[17]—that has sought (with rather spotty success) to engage in collective bargaining with CRM firms about wage rates, benefits, and retirement. If you think you'd just like to do archaeological research, and wouldn't mind doing it for somebody else, then hey-ho, it's a shovelbum's life for you.

Maybe. Before you decide, consider some statistics. The UAFT—admittedly not, perhaps, the most unbiased of sources—provides the following wage and hour data for the typical U.S. shovelbum:

> Average total hours worked per year: 1,400 (about 1/2 of a full time 9-to-5 job)

Number of months per year with some CRM work: 10

Average hourly wage: US$8.00/hr.

Average annual income (before taxes): US$11,200

The American Cultural Resources Association[18]—an organization of CRM firms and therefore more representative of management than labor, has estimated wages a bit higher based on a 1995 survey—about $8.60 an hour back then, and wages have certainly improved in the last ten years.[19] In most fieldwork situations you also get per diem—room and board. The better CRM firms, too, are anxious to keep good employees, and try to find ways to pay better salaries and to offer decent benefits packages. However you figure it, though, you're not going to get rich.

But the work is fun and exciting, right? Well, it depends on your perspective. You'll be working mostly outdoors, with the sun on your cheeks and the wind in your hair, but also often enough with the rain on your head and the mud sucking on your boots. The work should help you build up your muscle tone and keep your weight down, but you may also strain your back, pull muscles, and rupture tendons shoveling, pushing wheelbarrows, and schlepping buckets of dirt around; cramp your knees and twist your wrists spending hours crouched in the bottom of a pit troweling; fill your lungs with dust and pollen spores. Sometimes the places you'll work will be beautiful—wooded valleys, rugged mountains, sun-swept deserts—but it may be hard to deal with the fact that the reason you're working there, more often than not, is they're about to be transformed by construction, land development, or whatever else it is whose effects your bosses are trying to assess or mitigate. And the places aren't always very beautiful—you may well work in highway medians, vacant city lots, stinky bogs. You'll be stung by bees, bitten by snakes, chased by bulls, perhaps shot at. You may have to put up with bulldozers growling on the edge of your site waiting for you to get off so they can tear the place up. You'll spend your nights in cold, soggy tents or in cheap motels, most likely, and eat very few gourmet meals unless you put fast food and lentils in that category.

If all that's OK with you, though—if you're up for roughing it, and want the joy of discovery—maybe the closest thing to real exploration you can get in the twenty-first century without traveling off the planet or to the bottom of the ocean, or spending megabucks sailing off to the central Pacific or canoeing up the Amazon—shovelbumming can be a pretty rewarding thing to do for a while. I suppose my memory's tinted with the golden patina of age, but I can recall a good many lovely, starry desert nights and crisp mountain mornings, and days spent in honest labor along babbling Sierra Nevada streams and on beaches within salt-spray distance of the Pacific surf. And finding things, trying to puzzle meaning out of, or into, patterns of rocks and dirt and bones in and on the land. R. Joe Brandon, who runs Shovelbums.org, claims that every archaeologist worth his or her salt has gone through a shovelbum phase, and maybe he's right, if you define the term loosely enough. If nothing else, shovelbumming teaches you a lot about archaeology in the real world. It's also one of the few paying jobs you can get with an undergraduate degree in one of the social sciences; and as a source of stories to tell your grandchildren, it beats flipping burgers.

The Specialist

Finally, there are people who specialize in particular kinds of archaeology, or studies relevant to archaeology, who get hired or awarded contracts to perform specialized services. Some people work full time in curation facilities conserving artifacts and other material. Some work in labs doing things like radiocarbon age determination—measuring the age of organic things by measuring the relative percentage of different carbon isotopes they contain. Some work full time as historical researchers. Some specialize as writers of archaeological reports, others as managers of archeological projects or organizations. Joe Schuldenrein runs a whole company that specializes in *geoarchaeology*—the application of geological expertise to archaeological studies (called Geoarchaeology Research Associates, naturally).[20] There isn't space here to begin to list all the many kinds of specialists who get involved in archaeology, or who are employed full- or part-time working with archaeologists, but the *Archaeologist's Toolkit* provides a lot of detail in the volumes on Survey (Book 2), Excavation (Book 3), Artifacts (Book 4), and Archaeobiology (Book 5).

Special Opportunities

Which reminds me to beat a drum for archaeology by people with special skills and conditions, otherwise known as the handicapped or disabled. Long ago I had some kids from the California School for the Deaf who volunteered on a dig, and I was really impressed with how fantastically well they could concentrate on digging, and perceive fine distinctions in soil color, texture, and consistency. It got me to thinking about how many roles there might be in archaeology for people who relate to the world in special ways. The hearing-impaired person who's learned to use her eyes with greater sensitivity than other people, and hence can see things that the guy who hears normally can't. The person without vision who's developed great tactile sensitivity. The guy in a wheelchair who can organize and run a lab or curation facility. If you happen to have a disability, there may be things that you can do in archaeology better than anybody else; don't feel that you have to be able to ride a horse, hack through jungles, or dig holes all day.

The Race Thing

While I'm writing about people in different roles, with different characteristics, I might as well acknowledge the fact that by and large, in the United States at least, archaeology is pretty much a lily-white profession. There *are* African American, Hispanic, Asian American, and Native American archaeologists—in recent years more and more members of Indian tribes, in particular, have been going into archaeology or related fields, and the Society for American Archaeology runs a scholarship program to encourage their participation. And there are certainly Egyptian archaeologists working in Egypt, Chinese archaeologists in China, African archaeologists in Africa, and Indian archaeologists in India. But the fact remains that while the field has become relatively gender-balanced—if anything there are more women coming into professional practice in archaeology today than there are men—archaeology is by no means a racially balanced profession. This is worrisome, particularly since archaeologists so often work with the ancestral sites of nonwhite cultures, and we go through periods of soul-searching about why it's the case. I think the primary reason is that whether we like to acknowledge it or not, archaeology is something that only people with a fair amount of leisure time can afford to do. Until recently, that has limited its practice to elites in Europe and its former colonies. That's changing, but it takes awhile. Which means that right now, if you're not of European ethnicity and you're interested in archaeology, you're probably going to find lots of opportunities, a welcome mat rolled out by universities, museums, and consulting firms alike.

Other Important Roles

While we're considering roles, let's recognize that archaeologists don't work in a vacuum. We work with and otherwise relate to a wide range of nonarchaeologists all the time—with some of them so regularly that we ought to touch briefly on their roles in our work.

Colleagues in Other Disciplines

On the Earhart Project, I regularly interact with experts in oceanography, meteorology, forensic anthropology, historical research, radio science, aeronautics, materials science, metallurgy, and other disciplines. Much of my work in CRM is done in the context of environmental impact assessment, where I interact with biologists, water quality specialists, geologists, soil scientists, and engineers. I also work on a near-daily basis with historic preservation specialists whose training is in cultural anthropology, architecture, architectural history, landscape architecture, and planning. Nobody expects me to be an expert in these fields, and indeed I'd better not claim expertise beyond what I really have, if I want to avoid trouble with colleagues who really have such expertise. But I need to respect what my colleagues know and do, and to understand enough about their fields to know when to call on them for help and advice. For example, if I'm working on an environmental impact assessment and find that there's an old farmhouse that may be affected, I need to know enough to call in an architectural historian, and I should know enough about architectural history to find one who knows about old farmhouses in my region, rather than one who specializes in, say, Art Deco movie theaters.

Clients and Employers

Those of us who work as CRM consultants have clients to whom we're responsible—that is, the people and organizations who issue us contracts and pay for our services. Those who work in government agencies have organizational hierarchies to work within, which are very much like contractual clients in that they have specific expectations that archaeologists must meet. We need to respect such expectations, without being slavish about it. Sometimes the expectations of our clients or employers may conflict with what we understand to be our ethical responsibilities, or our responsibilities to colleagues or others, and we have to figure out how to resolve such conflicts, though in my experience really drastic conflicts are relatively rare.

Descendant and Other Associated Communities

If there are living people descended from those whose stuff we're studying, we need to pay close attention to their concerns—which may be dramatically different from ours. Documentable genetic descendants probably have definite legal rights, and often so do those whose association is more a matter of cultural affiliation than genetics. Even where science and written history may not support a claim of genetic or cultural affiliation, a modern group's belief that it has some association with a past group needs to be treated with respect; the modern group is, at the very least, made up of human beings with rights to their beliefs and cultural practices. In the United States, descendant groups are often federally recognized Indian tribes, which are sovereign nations in the eyes of the law, and have rights that are superior to those of states, local governments, and other organizations. Of course, other groups may also be associated with those we study—Chinese Americans have been very involved in archaeology in Sacramento, California's old Chinatown area, and African Americans have been deeply and effectively concerned about the treatment of New York's African Burial Ground.

Genetic descent and cultural affiliation aren't the only reasons that living groups may be concerned about the people and stuff that archaeologists dig up. The late Jan Hammil, founder of American Indians Against Desecration,[21] made the point forcefully to me back in the 1980s that many traditional Indian tribal people simply believe that they are responsible for the dead, regardless of "whose dead they are." The dead need to continue their journey to the spirit world, Jan argued, and it is the responsibility of the living to help them do so. We who muck around with the dead and their stuff need to respect such beliefs and consult thoughtfully with those who hold them, whether we share them or not.

Avocational Archaeologists

I was an avocational archaeologist—doing archaeology because I liked doing it, without getting paid—long before I got all my academic training and turned pro. Many people never make the jump to doing archaeology professionally, but are responsibly active in the field. Of course, there are many armchair archaeologists, who read about archaeological research but don't go into the field to actually survey or dig. Some avocationals do important research without doing fieldwork, through the study of previously gathered collections of artifacts and data, and through comparative historical studies. But most avocationals like to do some kind of fieldwork—surveys or excavations—and may do it on their own or through avocational archaeological societies, universities, and other programs. The Arkansas Archaeological Society,[22] for example, in cooperation with the state-sponsored Arkansas Archaeological Survey, runs a training program for its members, and issues certificates to people who achieve competency in site survey, excavation fieldwork, and lab work. Many other state and regional societies have similar programs. Avocationalists are active in virtually every country. Avocationalists are a powerful force in British archaeology, for instance, where the Council for British Archaeology[23] has eleven regional groups in England and affiliates in Scotland and Wales. In Israel, almost every kibbutz and farm town has an unofficial archaeological specialist, who often knows far more about the area's archaeology than do the professionals in Jerusalem and Tel Aviv.

Collectors

Some avocationals turn over everything they find to museums or other institutions; others keep them in private collections. Some professionals won't dignify private collectors with the title "archae-ologists," believing that the keeping of private collections is contrary to fundamental archaeological ethics. Others—and I'm in this camp—are less discriminating. It seems to me that if a person uses good archaeological methods, obeys the law, is careful to minimize the damage he or she does, reports his work, and respects the inter-ests of others, it's OK if he keeps the stuff he finds, though he certainly should provide for something responsible to happen to the stuff when he dies. People are fascinated by stuff from the past, and like to look at it and study it; we professionals ought to respect that fascination, particularly since we usually share it. In any event, there are lots of people who collect artifacts for a hobby, usually by doing surveys and surface collections, sometimes by digging. This is pretty generally illegal on federal and Indian land in the United States, but the laws vary widely with respect to other lands and in other countries, and often collectors focus their attention on sites that are being destroyed by erosion, farming, and construction. They can do good and important work, and I think they ought to be encouraged to do so—but I think I'm rather in the minority among my professional peers.

Pothunters, Traffickers, and Vandals

Then there are the people who dig up stuff without trying to use any kind of archaeological techniques, either for their own collec-tions or to trade or sell. These are the folks I'd call *pothunters*, though they may hunt for things other than pots (spearheads and arrowpoints, for example, or human skulls). Other archaeologists would classify all private collectors as pothunters. In my experi-ence there are relatively innocent pothunters who collect because they're just interested, don't keep good records just because they don't know how, and seldom if ever do anything destructive like digging up burials. On the other end of the scale are the real bad guys, who dig extensively, sometimes with heavy equipment, and are strictly in it for the bucks. They're often also involved in drug dealing and other illegal activities, sometimes carry weapons, and are best dealt with by law enforcement—assuming what they're doing is against the law, as it always is in the United States on fed-eral and Indian land, or on anybody else's land without the landowner's permission. Its illegality in other contexts depends on local, state, provincial, and pertinent national laws, which vary widely in what they prohibit and allow.

A rather special case is represented by people who dig up stuff to sell because they really, really need the money—poverty-stricken farmers in the midst of a drought in Peru, for example, or folks who are stuck in rural Mississippi without a job. What they do may be illegal, and archaeologists certainly think it reprehensible, but it's understandable in context. It's even more understandable when the stuff they're digging up was made by their very ancestors. The people of St. Lawrence Island in Alaska, for example, have been digging up and selling their ancestors' ivory and bone artifacts for generations, saying that the ancestors left them for their descendants to use. We archaeologists don't like the fact that they're digging the stuff up, destroying archaeological evidence in the process, but it's hard to fault them, given their depressed economic circumstances, or to argue with their logic.

Some pothunters, and some collectors, traffic in artifacts—that is, buy and sell them—as do some art dealers and other middlemen. The extent to which trafficking is legal depends largely on how the stuff trafficked is acquired; if the collector got it legally, it's usually legal to sell it.[24] Legal or not, trafficking is something that most archaeologists are very uncomfortable with, though some cooperate with dealers in, for example, authenticating stuff that dealers put up for sale. In some cases there are formal arrangements for the sale of artifacts from a site, more or less sanctioned by archaeologists. For example, Odyssey Marine Exploration[25] has done a detailed archaeological excavation of the S.S. *Republic* wreck site off the coast of Georgia in the Atlantic Ocean, and arranged for the sale of coins and some other manufactured items from the wreck after they're analyzed by the project's archaeologists. This sort of arrangement is quite rare at present, though I think it's likely to be more common in the future; generally speaking, archaeologists feel pretty antagonistic toward those who buy and sell artifacts. And a lot of traffickers in artifacts traffic in other things, too, like drugs.

Another group of archaeological site users toward whom archaeologists tend to be antagonistic are vandals—people who muck up sites just for the fun of it, or for other warped reasons of their own. The guy with the spray paint who scrawls obscenities or other "tags" on a cave wall's ancient pictographs (paintings), or blasts a panel of petroglyphs (inscriptions) with a shotgun. Or who finds a burial and smashes up the bones just to get a ghoulish kick. Most archaeologists (and I'll include myself in this group) feel that vandals ought to be—well, drawing and quartering is probably too merciful for them. Unfortunately, though, many archaeologists splash the label "vandal" on any nonprofessional who has the temerity to do anything with an archaeological site or its contents. This, I think, damns a lot of innocent people along with the guilty.

The Interested Public

Finally, there's the public in general, which has a great appetite for learning about and vicariously experiencing archaeology without ever doing it. Some archaeologists pretty much shun the public, but most of us welcome public interest, and those of us who work in CRM pretty routinely seek ways to relate our work to public interests. We put up explanatory signs around the sites we're working on, give tours, go on television, write popular accounts of our work, prepare videotapes and DVDs, even whole Web sites like the University of Texas's impressive Texas Beyond History.[26] We cooperate with The History Channel, National Geographic, the Discovery Channel, when they feature archaeology—which, of course, they often do—even if we're not always very happy about the products. We write pieces for *Archaeology* magazine,[27] published by the Archaeological Institute of America, and contribute material to the on-line Archaeology Channel.[28] Many of us are members of, or work closely with, avocational groups, and try to recruit members for them. Even if you're not much interested in interacting with the public, it's good to remember that ultimately, one way or another, the public pays the bill for what we do. It only makes sense to try to make our work relate to the public's interests.

Chapter Seven

Key Issues in Cultural Resource Management Archaeology

In bringing this book to a close, I'd like to outline some of the issues that we wrangle about in Cultural Resource Management-based archaeology, and encourage you to think about them. If I were an academic archaeologist, I'd probably be writing about the exciting frontiers of postprocessualism, or the implications of recent discoveries or research conclusions. But I'm a CRM guy, and the things that trouble my head, and the heads of those I work with, are related to our practice. I'm as interested as the next archaeologist in new research results or new ways of looking at theoretical problems, but it's the nitty-gritty CRM issues that I really *need* to think about. To encourage you to think about them, too, I'll phrase these issues in terms of hypothetical situations and questions. I won't provide any answers, because there aren't any that apply across the board; how the questions get answered varies from case to case and person to person.

To Dig or Not to Dig?

Let's imagine that the City of Shady Rock is planning a new sewage treatment plant, and there's an archaeological site—let's say it's a prehistoric village site with a cemetery—within the boundaries of the construction area. Should we propose salvage excavations, or are there other options?

If this project is in the United States, and there's some sort of federal funding or land or permits involved, the question of what to do with the site will be discussed during Section 106 consultation, and its treatment will probably be prescribed in a Memorandum of Agreement. The city's project manager may very well assume that the easiest thing to do is just get archaeologists to dig up the site and get it out of the way, and from the standpoint of archaeological research this may be true. Specialists in the archaeology of the area may be very happy to get their trowels into this site.

But from other standpoints digging the site may not be at all the best thing to do. In two recent cases in the state of Washington,[1] major projects have been halted and abandoned, at the cost of many millions of dollars, because they ran into archaeological sites (with cemeteries) that proved much more complex and significant than anticipated. Abandoning these projects wasn't the inevitable result of the discoveries, but in these two cases it was what happened, and the taxpayers lost a lot of money as a result. So digging the site may not be the best option from the standpoint of the client's pocketbook. And from the standpoint of a descendant community, or a community that regards itself as responsible for helping the dead continue their journey to the spirit world, it may be a tremendous affront to dig up the people buried in the cemetery.

There's also a research reason to consider doing something other than digging the site. A site dug and destroyed is a site that can't be studied in the future, except based on what's been dug out of it. If somebody comes up with a new question to ask, requiring information we didn't think to extract, she won't be able to ask it of our site. If someone develops a new technique for extracting data from a site, he won't be able to apply it to our site. And there's a finite supply of sites of any given kind, and they don't regenerate; for this reason, archaeologists often talk about archaeological resources being nonrenewable. So arguably, in order to bank archaeological data for future research, if we can feasibly keep a site in place, protected and unexcavated, that's what we should do.

So what are the alternatives, and how feasible are they? For example, is it possible to bury the site under fill, and build the plant on top? Would that cost less than digging? Would it work? Would it still be offensive to a community associated with the site? Would it really not damage the site? What about how the soil would be compacted by the construction? What about things that may happen in the future? What if the city decides, a hundred years from now, to construct a new fusion-powered poop purifier in the middle of the site, and its foundations will extend down through the fill into the old village?

Indirect Impacts

Suppose we're hired to do a survey in advance of construction on a new highway interchange, out in the middle of farm country. We find an archaeological site a short distance off the right-of-way of one of the roads flowing into the interchange. It won't be damaged by the construction, but it's a very safe bet that within a few years, because of the interchange, there'll be a gas station or a fast-food place or a box store built there that will wipe out the site. This kind of thing is referred to as an indirect or secondary effect of the project. What should we do? What should we recommend to the government agency responsible for the interchange project?

Many CRM archaeologists will say "nothing." "We can't do anything," they'll say, "because all we're hired to do is survey the interchange site, not the lands around it, and besides, the agency building the interchange doesn't have any jurisdiction over the adjacent lands, so it can't do anything about what may happen to the site."

But are these statements really true? Presumably we know what we were hired to do, but *should* we have been hired only to survey the interchange site? Doesn't the project proponent have the responsibility to consider all the effects of the project, including the indirect ones? That's certainly the case under U.S. laws like Section 106 and the National Environmental Policy Act. If the agency didn't know that when they hired us, shouldn't we have told them? Shouldn't we at least tell them now? And can the agency really do nothing about the site, just because it doesn't own it or otherwise have jurisdiction over it? If nothing else, couldn't it decide not to build the interchange, or to build it someplace else? Could it not try to persuade whatever local government has jurisdiction—and probably wants the interchange—that it ought to use its planning and zoning authority to protect the site? Has it really considered the environmental impacts of its project, and looked for ways to mitigate them, if it hasn't tried such options? Are we being responsible, either to archaeology or to our client's compliance with the law, if we don't suggest these things to the client? But what's the client going to say if we do?

Archaeological Versus Other Impacts

Now imagine we're hired by a telecommunications company to look at the archaeological impacts of a proposed new tower to hold wireless telephone antennas. The construction *footprint*—where the tower will be built—is only about fifty feet on a side, and we're able to be sure, after background research, a quick walkover survey, and a few shovel test pits, that there's nothing there of archaeological interest.

But the project site is a vacant lot in the middle of a neighborhood made up of old houses with pretty interesting-looking architecture, and the people of the neighborhood seem very proud of their neighborhood, and to really identify with it. The tower is going to be visible from all over the neighborhood. Shouldn't we say something about this to our client? Shouldn't the client be looking at the project's broad visual effects on cultural resources—like the neighborhood, which looks like it might be a historic district, and the people's perception of their identity, which might itself be a cultural resource? What's our responsibility here?

Here again, some contract archaeologists would say: "No, we're responsible only for looking at archaeological impacts, as we were told to by the client." And depending on what national, state or provincial, or local laws apply to the case, they might technically be right. But if we're going to sell ourselves as analysts of impacts on "cultural resources" or "historic properties," as most CRM firms do, shouldn't we pay some attention to such resources or properties, even if they're not archaeological sites? And have we done our client a service if we don't say something about the visual impacts, and when construction gets started there are suddenly irate neighbors out in force blocking the streets and beating up the construction workers—or filing injunctions?

One Site or Two? Or Three? Or . . .

You're doing a survey, and on one side of a creek you find an old living site. Lots of dark, greasy midden soil, maybe the remains of stone walls, housepits, animal bones and clamshells on the surface. Right across the creek—wow! There's a human skeleton eroding out of the creek bank, the skull looking right at you, and somebody's shoulder sticking out a few meters downstream. You pull out your notebook or PDA and start recording what you see.

So, do you call this all one site, or is the living place one and the cemetery another? And what about the pictographs (paintings on rocks) that you find an hour later when you climb the little hill southeast of the cemetery? What if the local elder who's accompanying you says that what's really important here is the marsh just upstream to the west, which is full of medicinal plants? When you plot this site on the map, where do you draw the boundaries?

This may seem like a petty sort of question, but you'd be surprised how exercised people can get about it. Do you lump everything together and describe it on a single (though perhaps rather complicated) site-recording form? Or do you split everything apart and do a form for each site? Your state or province or other administrative area probably has some kind of official site-recording system, and someone will have to assign permanent designation codes to whatever you record. Should they assign one code, or two, or more? What if the county or state or provincial boundary passes down the middle of the creek?

In a way it's all arbitrary, but in another way, whether you lump or split says something about how you view the archaeological universe, and the world of the past. Do we think of individual concentrations of stuff as sources of discrete information, or are we interested in how everything in the environment interrelates? Are we looking at the world through our own eyes, or are we trying to see it as people in the past did?

And your decision can have management implications, too. Suppose you're surveying in advance of a sewer line construction project. Suppose it's fifty meters from what looks like the edge of the cemetery to the first concentration of pictographs up on the hill. Does this mean it's safe to trench and lay the sewer pipe through the gap between the sites? Does it matter whether you say there's a gap between sites, or that it's all one site?

The Relevance of Our Research

We get a contract to excavate a site that's going to be taken out by a power plant. We've never worked in the vicinity before, but as far as we know, nobody else has either. What is our responsibility in terms of the data the site presumably contains? Should we try to get a representative sample of the site and write a good, solid, descriptive report? Or should we try to relate our excavation to some sort of significant research question in anthropology, history, sociology, or some other general theorizing discipline? Can we justify the expenditure of money—ultimately, money paid by the folks who buy electricity, in other words, the public—on just describing a site or the cultural group whose leavings it represents? On the other hand, aren't we being a bit hypocritical if we make up some big highfalutin' research question when we don't know whether our site will produce anything that might help us answer it? In other words, what should we do to justify the money that's being spent on our work?

Responsibility for the Stuff

We're negotiating a contract to excavate a big urban historic site—a place like Five Points in New York, or the Federal Triangle in Washington, D.C., once the famous red light district where the word hooker supposedly originated—in advance of government office building construction. We can be quite sure that the excavation will produce a whole lot of historic material—probably thousands of bottles, maybe millions of pieces of bottles. Jars, hair combs, tobacco tins, food containers, pistols, bedpans, you name it. There's going to be a lot of stuff that comes out of this site. What is our responsibility—and our client's responsibility—for taking care of this stuff?

In the United States the easy answer is: our client is responsible for making sure it's properly curated, by a proper institution, in perpetuity. Under the Archaeological Resources Protection Act (ARPA), that answer is legally correct if the land we're digging on is federally owned and the stuff is at least 100 years old and "of archaeological interest."

But perpetuity, as we observed in Chapter Three, is a long, long time. What's the practical implication of this curatorial responsibility? What's happened in the past, generally speaking, is that arrangements have been made for a properly equipped institution (maybe a museum, maybe a university, maybe a tribal curation center) to take the material and guarantee its perpetual care, taking an up-front per-unit fee. So we pay the institution, say, $200 per unit (box, cubic meter, whatever), which for, say, 100 units works out to $20,000, and the institution takes care of the stuff forever. In theory. But some institutions are beginning to say "wait a minute, it's costing us more and more to keep the lights on, the fire extinguishers charged, the security system going; to open the doors for researchers to work with the collections," and they're seeking to renegotiate their deals. Or they're saying "enough is enough," and getting out of the curation game altogether. How do we deal with this?

Do we persuade government to pump money into the creation of new curation centers? Do we find ways to cull the collections? Sell stuff we decide we don't need? Or is it a bad thing to encourage people to hold artifacts privately? If so, should we cull the collections and just throw things away? Destroy them? Or do we collect less in the first place? How do we do that, and what happens to the stuff we *don't* collect?

Repatriation and Reburial

A human skeleton washes out of a riverbank, on land controlled by a government agency. The coroner looks at it and decides it's not a recent murder victim. A radiocarbon test is run on a piece of rib, and it turns out the skeleton is very old—say 10,000 years if we're talking about somewhere in the Americas, maybe 20,000 in Europe, maybe 40,000 in Australia, whatever. There are indigenous communities in the area that have been there for a long time, but this guy is old enough that it's not possible to show a direct genetic link with any of them that's not shared with lots and lots of other groups. The skeleton is very interesting to physical anthropologists and biologists who study how human beings change and vary. Or maybe it's not so old but it's interesting for some other reason; maybe it looks like the guy died of measles, and there's been no prior evidence of measles in the area during the time he lived. What should be done with this skeleton?

A lot of physical anthropologists (though certainly not all) would say the skeleton ought to be curated in perpetuity for study; placed in a laboratory where it could be examined, measured, subjected to tests, including tests that today no one has even dreamed up. After all, twenty years ago we couldn't extract DNA from old bones; now we can. Who knows what we'll be able to do in another twenty, or fifty, or a hundred?

A lot of indigenous people, and other descendant groups (though certainly not all) would say that the skeleton ought to go back in the ground, with all proper ceremony, to continue its owner's journey to the spirit world. Or that it should be repatriated to them to re-bury or treat in some similar manner that they, as custodians of the ancestors, think is appropriate. They point out that this is how the ancestors of Euroamerican scientists are treated; why shouldn't their ancestors be treated in the same way?

Of course, in part the answer to this question depends on the law. In the United States the Native American Graves Protection and Repatriation Act provides for discovered human remains to be returned to the Indian tribes and Native Hawaiian groups with which they're affiliated, and there are similar laws in some other countries. But even if there is such a law, it may not be clear to which group the bones should go, and a U.S. Federal court has recently held that there has to be a pretty definite link between the skeleton and a living group in order for the group to get the body.[2] But in a larger sense, this is a question of good practice, and what we regard as our responsibilities as archaeologists. Are we more responsible to future researchers or to living descendants? And how does the dead guy himself fit into all this: do we owe *him* any consideration?

And what about artifacts associated with the body, or otherwise of cultural value to a living group? Should they go back to the group, or be kept somewhere for future study and exhibition on behalf of the whole human race? What if there's an engraved elephant bone on the skeleton's chest, and the indigenous group says that if it doesn't go back in the ground real quick it's going to bring fantastic misfortune to the tribe? But what if it's an African elephant bone, and the skeleton is found in Belize? How do you decide? And for that matter, who decides?

Avoiding Surprises

Our client wants to rebuild and expand a big highway bridge serv-ing an industrial area. She tells us that she doesn't care what the archaeology costs, she just doesn't want any surprises. This is actu-ally a quite common thing for clients to say, though you ought not take them quite at their word; if you tell them the archaeology will cost US$17 million and the project they're proposing will cost only

US$14 million to build, they'll probably balk. But surprises—finding something unexpected and awful enough to bring the project to a screeching halt in the midst of construction—are the bane of any project manager's existence, and they always want to avoid them.

One end of the bridge will be in the midst of an area that was leveled a hundred years ago and since then has been an industrial site; buildings have come and gone, the land's been churned up over and over again, and now it's just a great expanse of imported fill dirt and concrete. The imported fill is deep—say four to ten meters. The bridge footings, though, will go down through the fill into whatever lies below. Historical sources suggest that there used to be an indigenous village in the area, but that it was about 100 meters away from where the bridge footings will go in.

Here's the question: do we propose an extensive program of testing—removing big pieces of the fill to see what's underneath? Or do we do a little bit of testing and if we don't find anything that looks obviously significant, just monitor construction—that is, have archaeologists and representatives of the local indigenous group watch as the excavations are done for the footings? The testing option will be very expensive, and take a good deal of time; the monitoring option leaves the client with the risk of a surprise. But it seems like a low risk. What to do?

As I'm writing this, the Associated Press is reporting on one of the cases I mentioned at the beginning of this chapter, where this question was posed. The project involves reconstruction of a bridge at Port Angeles, in Washington State. To make a long story short, the agency and its archaeologists in that case chose the monitoring option, and it turned out to be a bad call. When the fill came off during construction—with monitors on hand in accordance with a Section 106 Memorandum of Agreement negotiated among the agencies, the State Historic Preservation Officer, and the concerned Indian tribe—burials began to appear. First a couple, then several, then scores, then hundreds, a giant cemetery, full of the ancestors of the living tribe. The tribe insisted that this was not at all what it had bargained for, and called for the project to be halted. At this writing, the agencies involved have decided to walk away from it, after having spent US$58 million on it. And it's not at all clear whether and how the bridge is going to get rebuilt.

Does this mean that the extensive, expensive testing option is the right way to go in every case? Surely not, but when and how do we decide when it is the right decision? And when we test, what kind of testing do we do?

Survey Standards

Our contract calls for us to "carry out the attached Scope of Work (SOW; Attachment 3)." Attachment 3 tells us to conduct a Phase 1B2 Archaeological Survey following the standards issued by the Historic Preservation Authority (in the United States, probably the State Historic Preservation Officer). The standards say that archaeological survey involves having professionally qualified archaeologists walk transects no more than 5 meters apart over the surface of the ground, inspecting the surface in detail and digging shovel test pits every 5 meters, passing the soil through screen no larger than one-quarter-inch in size . . .

Pretty specific, pretty directive, pretty detailed, but it may have nothing whatever to do with what the CRM laws require. In the United States, the Section 106 regulations are flexible, saying only that you've got to make a "reasonable and good faith effort" to identify historic properties that may be affected. A lot of State Historic Preservation Officers and archaeological organizations have decided that such an effort invariably involves spacing archaeologists X meters apart and having them march over the ground surface digging holes. There are several problems with this. First, it may not be necessary; depending on the nature of the proposed project and its likely effects, and the likelihood that sites will actually be in the area, it may be overkill. Second, it can come to be applied in such a rote manner as to become ridiculous. There are horror stories about crews spending days and days walking and digging shovel test pits in the top fifty centimeters of an area that is known to have been completely covered with imported fill fifty years ago to a depth of five meters. Third, it can distract us from what actually needs to be done to make a "reasonable and good faith effort" in a particular case. In one case, where the project may have extensive visual impacts but limited effects on the ground, archaeological survey may not be particularly relevant; what's really needed is an extensive identification of places where people may be troubled by what the project does to the view. In another case the main thing to do may be to talk with the elders in the local indigenous group. In a third, what may be needed is a really educated consideration of the landscape; in a fourth, a close look at the geomorphology. It all depends on what the project is, what kinds of effects it may have, what kinds of cultural resources it may affect. Doing a standard archaeological survey in every case puts the client at risk of failing to comply with the law, because she hasn't really identified the full range of cultural resources that may be affected.

But there are hundreds and thousands of projects going through the Section 106 review process in the United States all the time, and like numbers in other countries; we can't very well design our surveys *de novo* for each one, can we?

So there's the quandary. We need to tailor our identification work—our surveys or whatever else we do to find resources that may be affected by projects—to the specific needs of the project, the area, the types of resources and issues that may be involved. But there are so many projects that require surveys—or whatever—that such tailoring seems impossible to do. What's the answer?

Cooperating With the Bad Guys

Deepblue Sea Search plans to excavate the wreck of the *Zunkenschip,* a seventeenth-century cargo ship that went down a short distance off the coast. The reason Deepblue wants to excavate the wreck it to get the treasure that's reported to be aboard. Deepblue wants to hire us to work with them to make sure that the work is carried out according to archaeological principles and methods. Should we contract with them?

It's safe to say that the vast majority of archaeologists, inside and outside CRM, would say not just no, but hell no. Some archaeological organizations, in their codes of ethics, explicitly forbid cooperation with treasure hunters. Some officially exclude from their annual meetings anyone who's thus cooperated, and prohibit such cooperators from contributing to their publications.

A minority calls for a more nuanced approach. Let's work with the treasure hunters, they say, provided we can make reasonably ironclad arrangements to have the archaeology done right—that is, carefully, with full documentation, analysis, publication, and curation of everything that isn't sold. If we're concerned with the data, not the artifacts, they ask, why should it so freak us out if some of the artifacts go into private commerce after they're thoroughly analyzed?

Balderdash, says the majority. Treasure hunters are too intent on the bottom line, and the bottom line requires them to get the treasure with a minimum expenditure of their investors' money—assuming, of course, that they're not in the game just to rip off their investors, as most of them are. They'll never actually allow good archaeology. And besides, letting the artifacts go into private hands is a bad idea because we may in the future come up with new analytic methods that we'll want to apply to them, new questions we'll want to ask. And collections should stay together. You could cut up a Guttenberg Bible and sell it by the page, but it wouldn't be the same as the whole thing.

Come on, the minority replies. Do you really expect to come up with new techniques to apply to things like coins and gold ingots—the kinds of things that treasure hunters mostly put on the market? And in fact, dealers in such things keep better records of where they are than most museums do. Retaining data on where the stuff came from makes it more valuable, so there's a strong commercial incentive to keep good records. Doesn't it seem likely—particularly given how strapped most museums are for funds to finance curation—that if we ever need to do research on the ingots from the *Zunkenschip* we'll be able to get access to them in private collections at least as readily as we would if they were housed in an institution? An archaeological collection isn't a Guttenberg Bible, the minority argues; it's made up of individual, separate parts that routinely are separated from one another for analysis and display. And as to whether treasure hunters can ever, will ever do good archaeology, the minority goes on—they certainly won't if no archaeologist will work with them, will they? Why not try it, they ask, and see what we can do to create a commercial environment that supports good archaeology?

So what do you do? Your call.

Management and Labor

Imagine you're preparing a budget for an excavation project—a good-sized project in advance of some large-scale construction. It's a competitive situation, and while your proposal and those of rival firms will be compared and judged in large part based on merit (the client says, and you hope), price is going to enter into the equation, too. The less you can make your proposed work cost, the better.

You figure you're going to need to hire about 25 people to do the digging, and let's suppose you're not in a country where you just hire the folks from the local village—you're going to have to hire people on the open market. Since you want people with some experience and training—indeed, the scope of work insists on it— that means you're going to be hiring shovelbums. What do you budget for labor?

As discussed in Chapter Six, shovelbums are often pretty badly undercompensated, considering the kind of work they do. And the conditions under which they work are far from luxurious. You're sympathetic, and you want to get the best people, and have a happy crew, so you'd like to pay your folks well, make sure they're housed well, fed well, and otherwise taken care of. But that costs money, and you're pretty sure that some of your competitors will not be so attentive to their employees' interests, and still be able to hire crews. Jobs aren't that easy to find in this part of the world, and doing archaeology is more interesting than working at the carwash.

So what do you do? Budget enough to hire good people for good wages and treat them well, or go for the minimum to avoid being undercut by the competition?

Doing Another Discipline's Work

Let's say you're a prehistoric archaeologist in the United States— that is, you specialize in the archaeology of time periods before contact with Europeans. You're heading up a small team that's assigned to survey the site of a proposed housing development. Everyone on your five-person team is also trained in prehistoric archaeology at various levels. You find that there's a little old house on the project site, in which an elderly African American couple live. You know from looking at a coffee-table book about the vernacular architecture of the area—that is, architecture by people who weren't professional architects—that the house is a *shotgun* house. It's designed with doors at the middle of the front and back and a hallway between, so if you fired a shotgun in one door the shot would come out the other, assuming the gun had a pretty tight spread. Talking to the residents, you find that the house has been in their family for several generations.

That house might well be eligible for the National Register of Historic Places, as a good example of local vernacular architecture, and/or because of its association with local African American heritage. Your client obviously needs to know that, but you don't have the professional qualifications in architectural history or social history or cultural anthropology to offer an informed judgment. What do you do?

As usual, there's an easy answer to this one, but it's not necessarily as easy as it seems. You—that is, the company you're working for—ought to go get the appropriate expertise to make an evaluation. Hire an architectural historian and a social historian or anthropologist or sociologist. But that costs money and takes time, and your client's in a hurry, and if you ask for more time, and an increase in the budget, the client will be really unhappy and may balk, or at least may not give you another job. And hey, it's just one house, and anybody can see that it's a shotgun house. And maybe it's obviously been changed a lot over the years—windows replaced, aluminum siding attached—so it's lost integrity and therefore, arguably, *isn't* eligible for the National Register as a piece of architecture. And does this one family—this old couple—constitute a community with a history that's important to the region, or to anybody, really? Hell, you can put together an evaluation . . .

And maybe you can, and maybe nobody will have a problem with that, because although there are professional qualifications standards in the United States that most people in CRM try to follow, and that authorities like State Historic Preservation Officers try to insist are followed, they're not entirely binding. So as a matter of law it's not beyond the pale to have you as a prehistoric archaeologist evaluate a piece of architecture or an aspect of local social history. But on the other hand, maybe someone involved in review of the project *will* have a problem with your qualifications, and *that* could cause trouble for the client. And at a more visceral level, how do *you* feel about your ability to make the right call?

On still another hand, how do you feel about the abilities of the available architectural historians and other theoretically relevant specialists? The fact is that there are far more archaeologists working in CRM than there are other kinds of specialists, so you may not have a lot of experts to choose from. And you may know from experience that the most prominent local architectural historian is enamored only of stuff with columns on the front—high-style mansions and such; you can be sure he's going to say this scruffy little shotgun house isn't eligible for the Register. You see a lot about the house that's pretty interesting, like those hand-hewn timbers, and the details in the hall, but will he? And what about the residents and their history? You'd like to be sure the old couple and their extended family get a fair shake, but who's qualified to evaluate the house from the perspective of local African American history and culture? Nobody you know of. So how much of the evaluation do you take on even though it's outside what you're trained to do, and what can you do if you don't feel qualified to do it yourself?

What Makes a Site Significant?

You're working for a State Historic Preservation Officer in the United States, or a Ministry of Culture in some other country, and are responsible for making sure that significant archaeological sites in an area of about 2,000 square miles—a bit less than twice the size of the U.S. State of Rhode Island—are given a fair shake in development planning. There's a lot of development going on in your area, and it's very important to the economy. There are also lots and lots of archaeological sites—big ones, little ones; deep ones, shallow ones; sites with architecture and without. Old sites and not-so-old sites. Large occupation sites and short-term camps or farm plots. How do you decide which ones are so significant that you'll fight for their preservation at the expense of development foregone? Which aren't that significant, but are important enough to insist that they be carefully excavated before they're destroyed? Which do you think can be destroyed after just brief documentation and maybe some sample excavations? Which do you think can be destroyed without any study at all, and without even considering preservation in place? What's your basis for deciding?

This question lies at the heart of CRM, and sometimes it's easy to answer. Maybe the site you're trying to evaluate is a great big complicated one with cemeteries or impressive architecture or works of art, and has a major constituency—a descendant group, or a powerful organization of some kind. Any fool can plainly see that it's a significant site, that people are going to fight for. But what if it's not that kind of site? In parts of the western United States there are many, many *lithic scatters*—places where ancient people spent some time making tools or weapons from flint and chert and obsidian, leaving stone flakes and other debris scattered on or in the ground. How significant is each of these? How about a circle of rocks left from the long-ago erection of a tipi or some other kind of relatively ephemeral structure? What about nineteenth-century logging sites? World War II foxholes and trenches? Trash dumps from the time of the Great Depression?

As a CRM archaeologist you're likely to spend a lot of time trying to figure out rational, defensible ways of deciding on the significance or non-significance of sites like this. Maybe you'll try to establish some kind of arbitrary standard—five flakes per square meter means a significant site, say, and less than five flakes is not significant. Stone rings are significant enough to record, perhaps, but not significant enough to preserve unless there are a whole lot of them, or they're in really good condition. But such standards *are* arbitrary, and they may be hard to defend—either against the archaeologist who says that sites with very few flakes per square meter are critically important to his research, or against the land manager or developer who thinks it's outrageous to spend time and money worrying about a few flakes on the ground.

Or maybe you're not comfortable making decisions based on just what you can see of sites like these; maybe you'll want each one to be test excavated and maybe be the subject of other kinds of studies. But these studies take time and money, and before long you may find yourself causing agencies and developers to spend more time and take more trouble evaluating sites than they would if they just assumed everything was significant and moved on to figuring out management strategies. And, of course, spending a lot more time and taking a lot more trouble than they would if they decided they were all insignificant and let the 'dozers roll. You may find your boss urging you to find ways to speed things up, streamline, accommodate the developers. Your boss may find the governor urging her to do the same, or to can the tree-hugging obstructionist who's causing all the trouble.

So what else can you do? Is there a way to avoid getting trapped in arguments over site significance? Avoid getting steamrolled by the forces of economics and politics? Can you solve this problem before it becomes the source of a crisis?

Most of these riddles don't have right or wrong answers, though some are righter or wronger than others in different contexts, or are viewed in more absolute terms by some people than they are by others. If you practice archaeology in CRM, you're likely to have to confront many of them in your career, and many others. Good luck!

Chapter Eight

Conclusion: A View from My Backyard

Back in Chapter Two, I imagined my backyard as an archaeological site. That's the way you begin to think when you've been in archaeology for a long time—you imagine every place you go as it might appear a hundred or a thousand years from now. What will remain, what won't? What will have been transformed by weather, reuse and recycling, vandalism, natural and social change, and just plain deterioration? How will it have been transformed? How may archaeologists of the future interpret it? I suppose it's an odd way to view the world, but it does give you a degree of humility.

Being always aware of how the present morphs into the past, changing its form as it goes, also makes you realize how much we've lost from what's already in the past that can be depressing. Archaeology has become pretty sophisticated, and new analytical techniques are being developed all the time, but we still can reconstruct only a small fragment of what went on in the past, and there's something very sad about that. So many human accomplishments large and small lost to us; so many lessons learned but forgotten. So many things of beauty and interest gone without a trace, or leaving only the wisps and tatters that we can tease out of the ground.

Cultural Resource Management is largely about trying to preserve more than wisps and tatters. Trying to keep something of what we value today for cultural reasons, and what's been left to us from the past, for—in the words of the U.S. National Historic Preservation Act—"the inspiration and benefit of present and future generations."[1] That's the mission of archaeology in CRM, too, together with archaeology's traditional mission of ferreting out what the past has left us and figuring out what it means.

But of course, my family and I use our backyard, and continually transform it, often destroying the expressions of what it used to be like, our own small past accomplishments. Which is another fact of life in CRM. Life goes on, change happens, change is an inevitable requirement of life. Change is not a bad thing, even though it always destroys.

One of the nice things about archaeology as a component of CRM—one of the more realistic things, and probably one of the major reasons that in the U.S., it's mostly archaeologists who run the CRM firms and the Section 106 operations in the agencies and State Historic Preservation Offices—is that we're really not at all intent on stopping change from happening. We know we can't put Troy or Camelot or Five Points back together again and bring it physically, literally, to life, and we don't particularly want to. We want to learn what we can from what's left of it, tell its story, and retain what we learn as a record that can be consulted in the future, but we're not trying to keep the future from coming. The charge that we're trying to "stop progress"—often thrown at us by frustrated land developers and construction project managers—is a bum rap.

What we *do* want to do—what we want everyone to do—is look before we leap; don't light the fuse before we get an idea of what we're about to blow up. Don't get fixated on a particular way to address some legitimate societal need—by building the highway or stock pond, hospital or orphanage in precisely *this* location, designed exactly like *that*—until we've gotten a fix on what doing it that way will destroy, whether what will be destroyed is worth saving, and, if so, what can feasibly be done to save it. That takes a bit of time, but if we start early, and work cooperatively, it's time that can be scheduled in an orderly way. And it's time well spent if for no other reason than that it can avoid what every project manager hates worst of all—surprises.

If you're just getting started in archaeology, or thinking about getting started, and decide to practice in CRM, one of the things you're going to have to get used to is helping make decisions about what should be saved and what can be let go. You'll make these decisions quite directly and personally when doing fieldwork, every time you decide on what size excavation unit to dig, what gauge screen to use, how many soil samples to take. On a larger scale, the decision may not be exactly yours to make; it will probably be some more or less remote government authority who will decide whether a site is significant enough to be considered in planning, and that official or some other will probably decide whether in the end the site stays or goes. But your recommendation will probably have at least some weight. It will—we can hope—influence the decisions that others make.

In making such decisions and recommendations, the trick is to be realistic without becoming unprincipled or jaded. To work with the project proponents without becoming their toady. At the end of the day, to feel that your decisions have been responsive to the interests of future generations, recognizing that these interests lie both in preservation *and* in progress.

A lot of CRM people talk about having a responsibility to *the resource*—that is, to the sites and structures and buildings and landscapes themselves. I used to talk that way, but have come to think it rather silly. The resources don't care; the sites don't complain. What we're responsible to, I think, is the future, and what discharging that responsibility requires is achieving balance between saving resources and facilitating needed change.

But another thing to remember about CRM is that it's not just archaeology, and the decisions aren't just yours to make, or yours and the project managers'. You have colleagues in other disciplines to think about; the fact that you don't much care about the old building sitting on the site you want to dig doesn't mean it's not very interesting to the architectural historians. You have the requirements of law and the interpretations of its enforcers to think about; you have to make your decision in a manner that's consistent with the relevant laws and regulations, and responsive to the opinions of government agencies.

You have to consider the concerns of those who foot the bill—taxpayers, ratepayers, clients—and understand that they have a large and legitimate say in what's done. You have the people who administer the companies and agencies for which you work, who have to do things in a businesslike manner and concern themselves with corporate and bureaucratic survival.

And most of all, I think, you have to consider the interests of just plain people—the people who value what we call archaeological sites, those who treasure other kinds of cultural resources, and those who have other priorities. Particularly, I believe, we need to make room at the decision-making table for marginalized communities that are easily excluded—indigenous groups, people of color, low-income communities, people who fall outside the mainstream in terms of political power, education, religion, and culture. Most of us archaeologists in the United States and a lot of other countries, after all, call ourselves not only archaeologists but anthropologists, and it's to the communities with which we interact that anthropologists have our first and most profound obligations.

Many of us got into archaeology because we found it easier to get along with the dead than the living, but if we're going to practice CRM, we simply have to rearrange our preferences as best we can.

All that said, and acknowledging all the complexities of doing it both in the context of CRM and outside it, the poor pay and crummy conditions under which we often work—archaeology remains a field in which I think most of us feel privileged to work. If you didn't understand it already, I hope this book has given you some idea why this is so.

Appendix A

A Small and Unsystematic Sample of Archaeology-Related Worldwide Web Sites

About.com Archaeology: http://archaeology.about.com/

Advisory Council on Historic Preservation: http://www.achp.gov

American Cultural Resources Association: http://www.acra-crm.org/

Archaeology Magazine Online: http://www.archaeology.org/

The Archaeology Channel: http://www.archaeologychannel.org/

Archaeological Parks of the United States: http://www.uark.edu/misc/aras/

Archaeological Societies: http://archaeology.about.com/blmokebib3.htm?terms=Archaeology

Archnet: http://www.archnet.asu.edu/archnet/

Aviation Archaeology: http://www.tighar.org

Biblical Archaeology Society: http://www.bib-arch.org/

British Archaeology Magazine: http://www.britarch.ac.uk/ba/ba.html

Cabrillo College Archaeological Technology Program (training for archaeological technicians): http://www.cabrillo.edu/academics/archtech/program/index.html

Council for British Archaeology: http://www.britarch.ac.uk/

Current Archaeology (UK): http://www.archaeology.co.uk/

Cultural Resources: http://www.eculturalresources.com/index.php

English Heritage: http://www.english-heritage.org.uk/default.asp

Internet Archaeology (Council on British Archaeology): http://intarch.ac.uk/

Left Coast Press, Inc.: http://www.lcoastpress.com/

National Association of State Archaeologists: http://www.uiowa.edu/~osa/nasa/

National Conference of State Historic Preservation Officers: http://www.ncshpo.org/

Society for American Archaeology: http://www.saa.org/

Shovelbums.org: http://www.shovelbums.org/index.php

Society for Historical Archaeology: http://www.sha.org/

Archaeology of Texas (spectacular site): Texas Beyond History: http://www.texasbeyondhistory.net/

U.S. Forest Service Passport in Time: http://www.passportintime.com

U.S. National Park Service Links to the Past: www.cr.nps.gov

Links to American Archaeological Organizations: http://www.archaeology.about.com/gi/dynamic/offsite.htm?zi=1/XJ&sdn=archaeology&zu=https://www.ecommerce.saa.org/saa/staticcontent/staticpages/adminDir/affiliates.cfm

More links to all kinds of archaeology sites: http://archnet.asu.edu/.

Also see http://www.nationaltrust.org/help/links_archaeology.html

African American Archaeology Links: www.anthro.uiuc.edu/faculty/cfennell/bookmark3.htm/

Appendix B

Some Cultural Resource Laws and International Standards

National Laws

- Ancient Monuments and Archaeological Areas Act (United Kingdom)

- Antiquities Act (U.S.)

- Archaeological Resources Protection Act (U.S.)

- Australian Heritage Commission Act (Australia)

- Cultural Properties Protection Act (Japan)

- *El Ley General de Patrimonial Cultural de la Nación* (Mexico)

- National Historic Preservation Act (U.S.)

- Native American Graves Protection and Repatriation Act (U.S.)

International Standards

UNESCO Conventions

- Convention for the Protection of Cultural Property in the Event of Armed Conflict (1954) (The Hague Convention)

- Convention for the Protection of the World Cultural and Natural Heritage (1972)

- Convention on the Means of Prohibiting and Preventing the Illicit Import and Transfer of Ownership of Cultural Property (1970)

- Unidroit Convention on Stolen or Illegally Exported Cultural Objects (1995)

- Convention on Safeguarding of the Intangible Cultural Heritage (2003)

- Convention on Protection of the Underwater Cultural Heritage (2001)

UNESCO Recommendations

- Recommendation on International Principles Applicable to Archaeological Excavation (1956)

- Recommendation Concerning International Competitions in Architecture and Town Planning (1956)

- Recommendation Concerning the Safeguarding of the Beauty and Character of Landscapes and Sites (1962)

- Recommendation on the Means of Prohibiting and Preventing the Illicit Import, Export and Transfer of Ownership of Cultural Property (1964)

- Recommendation Concerning the Preservation of Cultural Property Endangered by Public or Private Works (1968)

- Recommendation Concerning the Protection, at National Level, of the Cultural and Natural Heritage (1972)

- Recommendation Concerning the Safeguarding and Contemporary Role of Historic Areas (1976)

- Recommendation Concerning the International Exchange of Cultural Property (1976)

- Recommendation for the Protection of Moveable Cultural Property (1978)

Notes

Preface

1. Compiled from data collected by the American Cultural Resources Association.
2. Larry J. Zimmerman and William Green, series editors, *The Archaeologist's Toolkit*, 7 vols. (Walnut Creek, CA: AltaMira Press, 2003).
3. A good place to start is with *Cultural Resource Laws and Practice: An Introductory Guide*, 2nd ed. (Walnut Creek, CA: AltaMira Press, 2004).

Chapter Two

1. I actually wrote an article about one of the coins I found, which shows how hard up I've been at times for things to write about. It's called "A 1937 Winged Liberty Head Dime from Silver Spring, Maryland," and it's Chapter 20 in *Thinking about Cultural Resource Management: Essays from the Edge* (Walnut Creek, CA: AltaMira Press, 2003).
2. For details of the Garbage Project, see *Rubbish! The Archaeology of Garbage*, by William L. Rathje and Cullen Murphy (Tucson: University of Arizona Press, 2001).
3. See *Amelia Earhart's Shoes*, by T. F. King, R. Jacobson, K. Burns, and K. Spading (Walnut Creek, CA: AltaMira Press, 2004), and www.tighar.org.
4. The more or less definitive work on the archaeology of the Drake landing place is Raymond Aker's *Report of Findings Relating to Identification of Sir Francis Drake's Encampment at Point Reyes National Seashore: A Research Report of the Drake Navigators Guild* (Palo Alto, CA: Drake Navigators Guild, 1976). Not the easiest book to find, however.
5. Battle of the Teutoburg Forest. See Peter S. Wells, *The Battle That Stopped Rome: Emperor Augustus, Arminius, and the Slaughter of the Legions in the Teutoburg Forest* (New York: W. W. Norton, 2004), for an excellent summary and extensive reading list.
6. For discussions of New Archaeology, positivism, and such, see Alison Wylie's *Thinking from Things: Essays in the Philosophy of Archaeology* (Berkeley, CA: University of California Press, 2002).
7. Testing hypotheses in Micronesia. You can read my major attempt at

this in *Pisekin Noomw Noon Tonaachaw: Archaeology in the Tonaachaw Archaeological District, Moen Island, Chuuk* (Carbondale, IL: Micronesian Archaeological Survey and Southern Illinois University, 1983).

8. Postpositivism. If you're up for heavy jargon, try Michel Foucault's *The Order of Things: An Archaeology of Human Sciences* (New York: Vintage, 1994).

9. For information on the African Burial Ground, visit http://www.africanburialground.com/

10. For the archaeology of Five Points, see http://r2.gsa.gov/fivept/fphome.htm

11. To visit the Petaluma Adobe, see http://www.parks.ca.gov/default.asp?page_id=474

12. To learn more about the wreck of the *Sussex*, see http://shipwreck.net/area4registered.html. You'll have to register, but it's free.

Chapter Three

1. From Jesse D. Jennings, *Glen Canyon: A Summary* (Salt Lake City: *Anthropological Papers of the University of Utah 81*, 1966).

Chapter Four

1. Karen Ramey Burns, *Forensic Anthropology Training Manual* (New York: Prentice-Hall, 1999).

2. Rebecca Yamin, ed., *Tales of Five Points: Working Class Life in Nineteenth Century New York*, 7 vols. (Westchester, PA: John Milner & Associates, 2000).

3. At 36 CFR 79—that is, Title 36, Part 79 of the Code of Federal Regulations, on the Worldwide Web at http://www.cr.nps.gov/aad/tools/36cfr79.htm

Chapter Five

1. For information on the National Register, visit http://www.cr.nps.gov/nr/

2. For information about collections management from the U.S. National Park Service, see http://www.cr.nps.gov/museum/publications/index.htm

3. For the text of this convention, visit http://portal.unesco.org/en/ev.php-URL_ID=17716&URL_DO=DO_TOPIC&URL_SECTION=201.html

4. Photos in montage: 1. McNear Building, Petaluma, California. *Photo by author*. 2. Abraham Lincoln's text of Gettysburg Address. *Source, National Archives and Records Administration*. 3. Yurok fishermen Raymond Mattz Sr. and Jr. with a 58-pound salmon. *Photo by Arnold*

Nova, Yurok Tribal Fisheries. 4. Panther Meadow, a Native American spiritual place on Mount Shasta in California, itself a spiritually significant mountain to Indian tribes. *Photo by author.* 5. Fairchild Tropical Botanic Garden, Miami, Florida. *Photo by author.* 6. Katin Nikkichinnap and his wife Nesema prepare to fish, Pis Iras islet, Chuuk. *Photo by author.* 7. Chinatown, San Francisco, California. *Photo by author.*

5. In other words, Title 36, Part 800 of the Code of Federal Regulations. For the text, visit http://www.achp.gov/regs-rev04.pdf

6. For information on SWCA, see www.swca.com

Chapter Six

1. To learn about Morven, see http://www.historicmorven.org/

2. JMA's Web site is http://www.johnmilnerassociates.com/profile.htm

3. Email to author, December 2004.

4. Goodwin & Associates has a Web site at http://www.rcgoodwin.com/

5. From an email to the author, December 2004.

6. Nancy's CRMS Web site is http://www.crms.com/

7. The Colorado SHPO's Web site is http://www.coloradohistory.org/

8. The Advisory Council's Web site is http://www.achp.gov

9. Claudia's Web site at the Wyoming SHPO is http://wyoshpo. state.wy.us/

10. For a general overview of the BLM's CRM program, see http://www.nifc.gov/

11. For information on the Forest Service's CRM program (called "Heritage" in the Forest Service), see http://www.fs.fed.us/recreation/programs/heritage/

12. For information about China Lake, see http://www.nawcwpns.navy.mil/

13. The definition of Archaeological Field Technician is at http://members.aol.com/UAFT/fieldtec.htm

14. Shovelbum-oriented Web sites include www.shovelbums.org, http://www.archaeologyfieldwork.com, and http://www.eculturalresources.com/index.php

15. Cabrillo's is the oldest and perhaps most accomplished of several such programs around the country. See www.cabrillo.edu/academics/archtech/program/index.html

16. *Shovel Bum: Comix of Archaeological Field Life,* by Trent de Boer (Walnut Creek, CA: AltaMira Press, 2004).

17. The UAFT's Web site is http://members.aol.com/UAFT

18. For information on ACRA, visit http://www.acra-crm.org/

19. An informal survey taken by R. Joe Brandon in 2005 indicated a range in entry-level wages from $9 to $18 an hour, with an average of about $12.

20. Joe's firm's Web site is http://members.tripod.com/geoarch/

21. American Indians Against Desecration doesn't really exist anymore, but its parent organization, the American Indian Movement, certainly does. See http://www.aimovement.org/

22. The Arkansas Archaeological Society's Web site is http://www.uark.edu/depts/4society/index.php?pages/home and the Society for American Archaeology provides links to lots of state, provincial, and regional societies at http://archaeology.about.com/gi/dynamic/offsite.htm?zi=1/XJ&sdn=archaeology&zu=https://ecommerce.saa.org/saa/staticcontent/staticpages/adminDir/affiliates.cfm

23. The Council for British Archaeology's Web site is http://www.britarch.ac.uk/, and includes links to its affiliated groups.

24. There's a discussion forum for artifact collectors, owners, and dealers at http://prosbb.com/

25. Odyssey's Web site is at http://www.shipwreck.net/

26. See www.TexasBeyondHistory.net

27. *Archaeology's* online version is at http://www.archaeology.org/

28. The Archaeology Channel can be accessed at http://www.archaeologychannel.org/

Chapter Seven

1. The two Washington State cases involved expansion of a sewage treatment plant in Blaine, on the Pacific coast near the Canadian border, and construction of a dock needed in rebuilding a bridge at Port Angeles, farther south. Both projects ran into ancestral tribal cemeteries, and both ultimately were halted.

2. The case in point, popularly referred to as that of Kennewick Man, has been the subject of a great deal of acrimonious debate, and is discussed in a number of books and journal articles. I particularly like Dave Hurst Thomas' book *Skull Wars: Kennewick Man, Archaeology, and the Battle for Native American Identity* (New York: Basic Books, 2001) as an even-handed treatment that puts the case in context, but it's a bit dated now. A book of essays from various perspectives about Kennewick Man—also known as "The Ancient One"—is in preparation for the World Archaeological Congress, and should available in early 2006.

Chapter Eight

1. Section 2(3).

Glossary

Adaptive use: putting an old building, structure, or other thing to a new use while preserving its significant features; an important part of modern historic preservation.

Archaeological site: Generally, a location of past human activity that is studied by, or that may be studied by, archaeologists.

Architecture: Something that people in the past made that's not so portable: a pithouse, a temple, a mound. Also a professional field of practice: architects practice architecture, designing things to be built in the here-and-now.

Artifact: Something that people in the past made—a pot, a spearpoint, a statue—that's more or less portable. One of the major kinds of stuff from the past that archaeologists study.

Burial: A buried human body—in a grave, a tomb, some kind of burial facility (which may be only a hole in the ground or a crack in the rocks). Or, the act of burying something—"the burial of Pompeii by Mount Vesuvius."

Contemporary: Something that happened at more or less the same time as did something else you're referring to. The Roman chronicler Pliny the Younger recorded the eruption of Mount Vesuvius that buried Pompeii and killed his uncle, Pliny the Elder; that's a contemporary account. A nineteenth- or twentieth-century archaeologist's account of the same disaster isn't contemporary.

Contract archaeologists: archaeologists who do work under contract with clients, usually agencies or firms that want to undertake some kind of project and need help managing its impacts.

Culture: The characteristics that make us human, and make us think of ourselves as different kinds of humans—members of families, communities, nations, organizations. Includes ideas and beliefs in our heads and the way they're expressed in speech, songs, stories, dances, and ways of organizing ourselves to live together, find or produce food, make war, build and maintain our communities. Also includes all the physical stuff that goes along with those ideas and beliefs—artifacts, architecture, art, computers, furniture. Also used to refer to the beliefs, ways of life, and stuff of a given group of people, in the present or the past—"Hohokam culture," "the culture of northwestern Idaho."

Curation: Caring for artifacts, ecofacts, and other archaeological material, as well as documents, photographs, and digitized data, in such a way that they don't deteriorate and are more or less available for future study.

Data: Information. Archaeological sites contain data, and archaeologists record and work with data.

Ecofacts: Stuff that comes from the natural environment but may be found in an archaeological site (or sometimes elsewhere) and that is useful in archaeological research. Examples include animals bones, shells, teeth, feathers, and feces; plant remains and pollen.

Excavation unit, or just *unit:* The hole or pit an archaeologist digs, though to be accurate, it may be a very shallow hole or pit if the site isn't very deep, and the term can also refer to just a part of the hole or pit. Maybe we start out digging two-by-two-meter units scattered across a site, but then decide we have to dig six of them together to expose a big piece of architecture or a burial place. Then we have a four-by-six-meter hole in the ground (sometimes called an area exposure), but it's still recorded as a cluster of two-by-two-meter units, and we usually record the stuff we find in it with reference to the boundaries of the units.

Expression: Something we can notice that reflects something else. We say that an archaeological site is an "expression of past human activity," because the stuff it contains, and the way that stuff is organized in and on the ground, reflects whatever it is that went on there in the past.

Feature: A nonportable or not very portable thing in a site that we record because we think it may mean something. A feature may be architectural— a housepit, a foundation, a wall—or it may be something else—a storage pit, a firepit, a ditch, a pile of rocks. We may not know exactly what it is, or what it means. Maybe it's a patch of earth that's a different color than the ground around it, or that has a different texture or consistency. We may have no idea why it's like that, but we'll record it as a feature, take notes on it, take samples from it, and try to figure out what it is, or was.

Historic preservation: Narrowly, the management of historic places such as old buildings and structures, districts made up of old buildings and structures, culturally important landscapes, battlefields, and archaeological sites. More broadly, as used in the U.S. National Historic Preservation Act, not only the management of all such places but their identification, documentation, use in research and education, and consideration in planning.

Human remains: Human bones, mummies, cremated bodies, body parts. The human skeleton is full of information, about the age, sex, health, and even life activities of the person whose skeleton it is, and through analysis of DNA that can be extracted from bones and teeth, about the relationships between a given skeleton and other people, living and dead.

In situ: The Latin term used to describe something in its location, where we find it. We almost always excavate a feature in situ, and record it that way, before taking it apart to see what it's made of.

Marshalltown trowel: The preferred hand tool of most archaeologists in the United States and some other areas. A very high-quality, small-bladed mason's pointing trowel.

Midden: organic soil representing decomposing organic waste.

Overburden: Soil with little or nothing in it of archaeological interest, lying on top of soil or something else that i of archaeological interest.

Paleoenvironmental data: Information indicating what the environment used to be like in the past.

Pothunters: A pejorative term for people who dig up or pick up artifacts for their private collections or to sell, trade, or otherwise use for their own purposes. Some archaeologists put virtually all artifact collectors in this category; others reserve the term for those who are more or less wantonly destructive. A pothunter doesn't necessarily hunt only pots; he or she can hunt for any kind of artifact, or for human remains and other things left from the human past.

Predictive model: A set of predictions, generally displayed in graphic form on hard-copy or digitized maps or map overlays, about where various kinds of archaeological phenomena—such as sites of different types, or from different periods—are likely to be found.

Repatriation: the return of ancestral physical remains and/or cultural items to the tribes or groups with whose ancestors they're associated.

Rescue archaeology: In Great Britain and elsewhere, archaeological research performed in a hurry on sites about to be (or being) destroyed, to "rescue" threatened data and stuff.

Salvage archaeology: In the United States and some other countries, the same thing as "rescue" archaeology.

Screen: We often put the soil we take out of an excavation unit through a screen—usually one built for the purpose out of wood or metal and wire mesh that's coarser than windowscreen; in the United States, one-quarter-inch and one-eighth-inch mesh are the norms, though we use finer screens where we're looking for really small stuff, and to characterize soil samples in terms of grain size. The word is also used as a verb: "We'll screen everything from unit 17B through one-eighth-inch screen."

Shovelbums: Archaeological field technicians who travel from project to project and make up the skilled labor force that archaeologists draw upon to get the field and laboratory work done.

Site: We often use the word *site* as shorthand for *archaeological site*. That's really not correct, of course. A "site" is really just a place—any place, though it's usually a place where something happened, or something is, or was, or that we distinguish in our minds somehow from other places. "The site of the World Trade Center," for example.

Stratigraphy: Layers in the soil, a sequence of *strata*. As a general rule, deeper strata are older than shallower ones.

Stratigraphy, horizontal: A sort of confusing term that refers to how stuff can get sorted horizontally over the land surface through time. Maybe 2,000 years ago people live on a site for a while and then move away. Fifteen hundred years ago people return to the site—maybe the descendants of those who lived there before, maybe somebody else—but they don't set up shop on exactly the same place as people did before; they're a bit off to one side. The stuff that they leave may overlap or mix with the stuff left by the earlier people, or maybe it's doesn't. When an archaeologist comes along and studies the site, he or she is going to need to sort out the older stuff from the younger, but there may be no vertical difference between them—they're all on more or less the same horizontal plane or slope. The horizontal differences between the older and younger deposits are what we're talking about when we refer to horizontal stratigraphy.

For Further Reading

There are thousands of books about archaeology—archaeology in general, archaeological methods, the archaeology of this continent and that. There are mystery novels built around archaeology, stories of archaeologists' adventures digging here, surveying there. Biographies and autobiographies of famous archaeologists. I can't begin even to know them all, let alone list them. But here are some that are fairly current (i.e, in print), fairly general, mostly about how archaeology is done, that may give you some places to start.

Archaeology

Ancient North America: The Archaeology of a Continent. Brian M. Fagan. New York: Thames & Hudson, 2000.

Archaeological Method and Theory: An Encyclopedia. Linda Ellis. New York: Garland Publishing, 1999.

Archaeological Survey (Manuals in Archaeological Method, Theory and Technique). E. B. Banning. New York: Plenum, 2002.

Archaeology. David Hurst Thomas. Belmont, CA: Wadsworth Publishing, 1997.

Archaeology and Prehistory. Pam J. Crabtree and Douglas V. Campana. New York: McGraw-Hill, 2001.

Archaeology: The Comic. Johannes H. N. Loubser. Walnut Creek, CA: AltaMira Press, 2003.

Digging up the Past. John Collis. London: Sutton Publishing, 2001.

Discovering Our Past: A Brief Introduction to Archaeology. Wendy Ashmore and Robert J. Sharer. New York: McGraw-Hill, 1999.

Dug to Death: A Tale of Archaeological Method and Mayhem. Adrian Praetzellis. Walnut Creek, CA: AltaMira Press, 2003.

Field Methods in Archaeology. Thomas Hester, Harry Shafer, and Kenneth L. Feder. New York: McGraw-Hill, 1997.

Frauds, Myths, and Mysteries: Science and Pseudoscience in Archaeology. Kenneth L. Feder. New York: McGraw-Hill, 2001.

Handbook of Archaeological Methods. Edited by H. D. G. Maschner and Christopher Chippindale. Walnut Creek, CA: AltaMira Press, 2005.

In the Beginning: An Introduction to Archaeology. Brian M. Fagan. Upper Saddle River, NJ: Prentice-Hall, 2000.

Indigenous Archaeology: American Indian Values and Scientific Practice. Joe Watkins. Walnut Creek, CA: AltaMira Press, 2001.

Life in the Pueblo: Understanding the Past through Archaeology. Kathryn A. Kamp and Amy Henderson. Long Grove, IL: Waveland Press, 1997.

Lessons from the Past: An Introductory Reader in Archaeology. Kenneth L. Feder. New York: McGraw-Hill, 1998.

Linking to the Past: A Brief Introduction to Archaeology. Kenneth L. Feder. London: Oxford University Press, 2004.

Motel of the Mysteries. David Macaulay. Boston: Houghton Mifflin/Walter Lorraine Books, 1979.

People of the Earth: An Introduction to World Prehistory with CD. Brian M. Fagan. Upper Saddle River, NJ: Prentice-Hall, 2003.

Shovel Bum: Comix of Archaeological Field Life. Trent de Boer. Walnut Creek, CA: AltaMira Press, 2004.

Skull Wars: Kennewick Man, Archaeology, and the Battle for Native American Identity. David Hurst Thomas. New York: Basic Books, 2001.

The American Archaeologist: A Profile. Melinda A. Zeder. Walnut Creek, CA: AltaMira Press, 1997.

The Archaeologist's Toolkit. Edited by Larry J. Zimmerman and William Green. Walnut Creek, CA: AltaMira Press, 2003.

The Bluffer's Guide to Archaeology: Bluff Your Way in Archaeology. Paul Bahn. London: Oval Books, 1999.

The Complete Idiot's Guide to Human Prehistory. Robert J. Meier. East Rutherford, NJ: Alpha Books, 2003.

The Complete Idiot's Guide to Lost Civilizations. Donald Ryan. East Rutherford, NJ: Alpha Books, 1999.

The Order of Things: An Archaeology of Human Sciences. Michel Foucault. New York: Vintage, 1994.

The Past in Perspective: An Introduction to Human Prehistory. Kenneth L. Feder. New York: McGraw-Hill, 2003.

Thinking from Things: Essays in the Philosophy of Archaeology. Alison Wylie. Berkeley, CA: University of California Press, 2002.

Uncovering Australia. Sarah Colley. Sydney, Australia: Allen & Unwyn, 2002.

For fun reads, try *The Anasazi Mysteries,* by Kathleen and Michael Gear (New York: Tor Books, 2001, 2002)—mysteries set half in the ancient American Southwest, half among a crew of CRM archaeologists.

Cultural Resource Management

And if you're interested in reading about Cultural Resource Management, including but not limited to its archaeological aspects, I'll recommend my own books:

Cultural Resource Laws and Practice: An Introductory Guide. Walnut Creek, CA: AltaMira Press, 2004 (first edition, 1998).

Federal Projects and Historic Places: The Section 106 Process. Walnut Creek, CA: AltaMira Press, 2000.

Places that Count: Traditional Cultural Properties in Cultural Resource Management. Walnut Creek, CA: AltaMira Press, 2003.

Thinking about Cultural Resource Management: Essays from the Edge. Walnut Creek, CA: AltaMira Press, 2002.

And some others worth reading:

Claiming the Stones/Naming the Bones: Cultural Property and the Negotiation of National and Ethnic Identity (Issues & Debates). Edited by Elazar Barkan & Ronald Bush. Los Angeles: Getty Research Institute, 2003.

Cultural Property Law: A Practitioner's Guide to the Management, Protection, and Preservation of Heritage Resources. Sherry Hutt, Caroline Meredeth Blanco, Walter E. Stern, and Stan N. Harris. American Bar Association, Section of Environment, Energy, and Resources, 2004.

Cultural Resources Archaeology. Thomas W. Neumann and Robert M. Sanford. Walnut Creek, CA: AltaMira Press, 2001.

Legal Perspectives on Cultural Resources. Edited by Jennifer R. Richman and Marion P. Forsyth. Walnut Creek, CA: AltaMira Press, 2003.

Tribal Cultural Resource Management: The Full Circle to Stewardship. Darby C. Stapp and Michael S. Burney. Walnut Creek, CA: AltaMira Press, 2002.

Travel Guides

Finally, there are tour guides if you want to visit archaeological sites, many, many on the Worldwide Web, and some books; here are some U.S. examples:

Ancient Ruins of the Southwest: An Archaeological Guide. David Grant Noble. Flagstaff, AZ: Northland Publishing, 1998.

Archaeology Parks of the Upper Midwest. Deborah Morse-Kahn. Lanham, MD: Roberts Rinehart Publishers, 2003.

Those Who Came Before: Southwestern Archaeology in the National Park System. Robert Lister. Tucson, AZ: Southwest Parks and Monuments Association, 2nd edition, 1993.

Index

About the Author

My mother, the late Helen Fulling King, was responsible for getting me started in archaeology at age five, when she misadvised me that archaeologists had dug up the data upon which Walt Disney's portrayal of dinosaurs in the just-released film *Fantasia* was based. A strange bit of misinformation, since she'd been working on her master's degree in micropaleontology when my father swept her away into marriage and family life. With the help of friendly librarians in my home town's public library (a handsome Carnegie affair, now on the National Register of Historic Places and reused as the city museum), it took me only to the age of ten to learn my mother's error, whereupon I had to make an agonizing

The author with two tools of the archaeologist's trade: the Marshalltown Trowel and the Gradall. *Photo courtesy Dr. Hiro Kuroshina, University of Guam.*

decision about which way to go—fossils or ancient cultures. Obviously I chose the latter, and with dalliances here and there (writing, commercial fishing, the navy) I've been at it ever since.

But in about 1966, as an undergraduate at San Francisco State University (then College) surviving on the GI Bill and work in salvage archaeology, I fell in with a remarkable fellow student named Eric Barnes, who mixed art and urban planning with anthropology in his creative brain, and he introduced me to a law just signed by President Lyndon Johnson—the National Historic Preservation Act. Eric felt that it might be used to preserve and manage archaeological sites, rather than simply to get them dug up before they were destroyed. He convinced me, and my career lurched away from mainstream academic archaeology into what we now call cultural resource management or CRM.

Over the next ten years I oversaw the UCLA Archaeological Survey, helped set up the Archaeological Research Unit at the University of California, Riverside, and completed a PhD there in anthropology, did fieldwork in California's North Coast Range, Sierra Nevada, and Mojave and Colorado Deserts, and along the Pacific coast from Los Angeles north to the Oregon border. I set up a private consulting firm in northern California, took part in litigation, helped organize the Society for California Archaeology, and helped coordinate a legislative effort that would have established a state archaeological survey, modeled on one in Arkansas, had the legislation to create it not fallen to a veto by Governor Ronald Reagan. Becoming unemployable in California, I was enabled by the late, great New York state archaeologist Marian White to shuffle across the continent to Buffalo to set up a contract archaeology program for the New York Archaeological Council. I lasted a bit over a year on the Niagara Frontier before being recruited by the National Park Service to help write regulations and guidelines for the newly enacted Archaeological and Historic Preservation Act. I was a bit over a year in Washington, D.C., before being "detailed" to Saipan in the Northern Mariana Islands to help the Trust Territory of the Pacific Islands with its historic preservation programs. A tough job, but somebody had to do it.

Returning to the mainland in 1977, having established a pattern of employment suggesting that I'd never work anyplace for more than two years at a time, I was honored to be asked by the Advisory Council on Historic Preservation to head the office that nagged federal agencies nationwide about compliance with Section 106 of the National Historic Preservation Act. This took me back to Washington, where I actually worked for ten years with the council, through the Reagan administration and the beginning of Bush I. Policy disputes then led me to quit and go back into private practice, where I remain to this day. At various times in the last sixteen years or so I've worked intensively for agencies like the General Services Administration, the Department of Defense, and the Farm Service Agency in the Department of Agriculture, and consulted a good deal with Indian tribes and Native Hawaiian groups, besides authoring several textbooks and a number of journal articles on CRM topics. I've taught short classes for the University of Nevada, Reno, and the National Preservation Institute, and now both teach and consult with SWCA Environmental Consultants (www.swca.com). And I've returned to archaeology as the volunteer Senior Archaeologist on The International Group for Historic Aircraft Recovery's Amelia Earhart Search Project—read all about it at www.tighar.org or in *Amelia Earhart's Shoes* (AltaMira Press 2004).

I welcome comments, criticisms, questions, and debate about what I say in my books and articles, though I'm not always the most prompt of correspondents; teaching and consulting keep me on the road a lot. I can be contacted, most of the time, at tfking106@aol.com.